THE STREETS
tower blocks & top tens

THE STREETS

tower blocks & top tens

by jimmy ramsay

Independent Music Press

Published in 2005 by
INDEPENDENT MUSIC PRESS
Independent Music Press is an imprint of I.M. P. Publishing Limited
This Work is Copyright © I. M. P. Publishing Ltd 2005

The Streets: Tower Blocks and Top Tens by Jimmy Ramsay

British Library Cataloguing-in-Publication Data.
A catalogue for this book is available from The British Library.

ISBN 0-9539942-8-7

Cover Design by Fresh Lemon.
Edited by Martin Roach.

Printed in the UK.

Independent Music Press
P.O. Box 69, Church Stretton, Shropshire SY6 6WZ

Visit us on the web at: www.impbooks.com

For a free catalogue, e-mail us at: info@impbooks.com
Fax: 01694 720049

Dedicated to The Blue Boy and his mom.

INTRODUCTION

'Sheila's ever so good with colours. I never liked what the other girl did, you know, the one with the funny eye. I always wore a hat when I came home. I think I'm going to buy that song about cry your eyes mate, it's always on in Supercuts. In fact, I think I'll buy his album, bet it's ever so lovely. Oooh, he's got such a way with words.'

There, in my kitchen, at that precise moment in my life, The Streets went mainstream.

My mom, freshly washed-coloured-and-blow-dried, wanted to buy a copy of *A Grand Don't Come For Free*, Mike Skinner's sophomore album, a concept piece concerned with the urban decay festering around the life of one particular anti-hero and his mundane yet epic personal battles. With the words 'cunt', 'fucking' and 'smoking crack' in the lyrics, among numerous other 'phrases' Mom probably didn't use down Supercuts.

'It's not all like 'Dry Your Eyes', Mom, there's some pretty dark stuff on that record.'

'Oh, I know, that's kind of his 'ballad'. Beryl told me. Anyway, you forget, I bought a copy of Cliff Richard's 'Devil Woman', so I know all about dark ...'

She bought the album.

She loved it.

She said he probably didn't need to swear as much, but the girl was no good for him anyway.

It was late 2004. My record-listening world had just entered hyper-reality. Coincidentally, and on a somewhat grander scale, Mike Skinner's life would never be the same again either.

I wasn't alone of course. Mike Skinner's 'modern classic' 'Dry Your Eyes' had been the moment when most of Britain could say they knew that there was really only one person in The Streets. They knew who he was. It had been building for some time, and that particular radio-friendly, heard-in-Burtons-and-Asda masterpiece was actually just the culmination of years of creative gestation. It had been a long and slippery climb, but somehow, Mike Skinner's single was at Number 1 in the charts.

And because of people like my mom, so was his album.

CHAPTER 1:
STREET'S LIFE

'You know, a lot of journalists are quite posh. What are the big papers called? Y'know, the ones that are physically big?' Broadsheets. 'Yeah. Those journalists are a bit posh. They see me as this working class urchin, and I'm really not. I was quite well raised.'

Mike Skinner.

Birmingham at the turn of the Millennium: the second city was the recent recipient of hundreds of millions of pounds of development funds to revitalise its tired façade and serve a hair-of-the-dog to the post–War hangover which had clouded the city's skies for nearly sixty years. Within what seemed a few short months, Brum was being touted as a 'city of culture', with theatres, restaurants, a shopping centre the size of most towns and a growing reputation as the UK's cosmopolitan 'dark-horse'.

When Mike Skinner was born there in the late 70s, Birmingham was a shit-hole.

Back at the start of Thatcher's Britain, Birmingham was everything that a modern city wasn't supposed to be. Swathes of modernist architecture – hastily injected onto the landscape to repair the work of German bombers – had turned many of the arcades and estates into a mugger's paradise. Unemployment was high, morale was low, the staple industries that had given birth to the aorta of the Industrial Revolution – cars, metal work, engineering etc – were closing down faster than a bankrupt's credit record. The football teams offered brief respite from the mundanity, but even Aston Villa and WBA's early 80s brush with success was fleeting.

The Midlands was not a complete cultural vacuum. There were beacons of hope, such as Coventry's Two Tone scene and bands such as The Specials and The Selecter. However, even this was a product of rebelling against the very same social depravation and anti-Thatcher sentiment that was also rife in Birmingham. Yet those few tarmacadam-ed miles that distanced these two Midlands sisters might as well have been a few thousand. Birmingham in the late 70s was no fun.

The city back then could bestow few positive things on its inhabitants ('Birmingham's quite average, it's not a city of opportunity,' says Skinner), but one guaranteed attribute was the accent. Dense, dry and at times incomprehensible to anyone living outside of the West

Midlands. The Brummie accent is filled with tones that sound bored with life even when describing the happiest day. And, let's be blunt, it solicits a preconception from any outsiders that the person talking to them is thick. I know from personal experience – I was born and bred only a few miles from Skinner's home in a part of the Black Country so introverted that the spoken word makes no sense even to Brummies. Skinner himself has compared the accent to the American Deep South, *The Simpsons'* Cleetus without the redneck, if you like.

"When Mike Skinner was born there in the late 70s, Birmingham was a shit-hole."

Given the social significance which has been injected into The Streets' Mike Skinner's latterday work by an impressed media, it is to his credit that he has chosen not to mythologize his childhood. It is a temptation that many stars cannot resist, especially when an exaggerated poverty or dramatised family situation can sell more records. Skinner, perhaps typically bluntly, says he was neither working-class nor middle-class, but instead the archetypal child living in the relatively new-build, red brick, cookie-cutter house made in their millions, the garden-front-and-back, lounge-through-diner template which is to architecture what Bernard Manning is to multiculturalism. He was, in his own words, 'Barratt-class: suburban estates, not poor but not much money about, really boring.' He has never claimed to be 'ghetto'.

With refreshing honesty, Skinner repeatedly shuns any opportunity to ghetto-ise his history: 'I did not have a hard life: my parents always had jobs, and they stayed together, and they never beat me up. You know what I mean? We didn't live in a shitty house.' He wasn't trapped eighty feet up in the smog in a urine-laden, drug-infested tower block that litter his album artwork and videos; he lived in a decent house in a decent area. Not posh, but certainly not inner city. But then, Skinner has never pretended otherwise. Some would argue that without emotional or actual conflict or difficulty there can be no creativity ('Great artists suffer for the people':

> *"School was hard. It's quite tough for boys — you have to establish yourself as someone not to be fucked with, and I was never good at that."*

Marvin Gaye) but it would be exactly these ordinary, everyday machinations of Skinner's life would provide the very grist for his mill that made him such a success (more of which later).

Mike Skinner was the youngest of four children born to relatively older parents, originally from London. His father, in his seventies by the time Mike was topping the charts, is said to have once carried an unexploded bomb into a police station during the Blitz, handed it over the counter and walked away unscathed (no lyric battle puns about 'dropping bombs' please). Maybe he could see inside; he did, after all, sell X-ray machines for a living. Mike would later credit his 'good salesman' skills to his father's chosen line of work.

Mike grew up in the south of Birmingham within

this family of Londoners, an odd mix of Cockney and Brummie (Brockney sounds better than Cummie). The point being he had the nation's two biggest cities indelibly inked into his psyche even as he grew out of short trousers. That acute insight into inner-city life – not necessarily a deprived one, just an urbane existence – would provide him with enough lyrical fodder to last a lifetime.

Mike Skinner knew he wanted to be involved with music from the age of five, when he would make little more than random noises on the family keyboard. By the time he turned nine, his enjoyment of fiddling about with keyboards had evolved into an ambition to actually make and work in music.

First up was school. Although he didn't have to walk through metal-detectors at the school gates, Skinner says his education had its moments. 'Not hard, not easy,' he would later tell *Interview* magazine's Ray Rogers. 'School was hard. It's quite tough for boys – you have to establish yourself as someone not to be fucked with, and I was never good at that. I wasn't at the rock bottom of the stack – I wasn't a freak – but I was nowhere near the top. And it's hard at that age. If you're on the football team, or play other school sports, it makes you physically confident, and I was never really into that.'

What he *was* into, was music. Not the 'music' they taught at school – all classical composers and sight-reading – but American urban music, specifically hip-hop. He cherished his copy of the Beastie Boys' 'Rock Hard EP' and 'She's Crafty'; his favourite hip-hop album is Nas' *I Am ... The Autobiography*; he later worshipped Snoop too. Inevitably, this fascination with listening to music quickly turned into a curiosity to actually make it. Mike had an early dalliance with a guitar but this was quickly shelved in favour of those keyboards and, fairly soon after, some tape decks.

When his pre-teens beckoned, he turned his small bedroom into a mecca to rap, complete with posters of his heroes and even going so far as to 'sound-proof' his little den with an old mattress. The cupboard made a crude studio booth. With the tape machines and this impromptu set-up, the young Mike Skinner started to roughly record his own mixes.

His brother's Run DMC albums were always a primary source of inspiration: 'I used to record the intros from songs, from before they started rapping, onto another tape and then record them over and over again, so it kind of looped. And then I would rap over it and record that back into another tape recorder.' Although Mike says these fumbling forays into mixing were 'awful', it was nonetheless here that the seeds of what would become The Streets were sown.

He sank ever more heavily into US hip-hop. This genre that had originally been ignored on a disgracefully comprehensive scale by most music television stations, popular radio play-lists and major city venue circuits, but by the mid-90s, it was on its way to becoming the biggest selling genre in the world.

Like most artists, Skinner's first forays into music might seem a tad embarrassing when looked back on standing next to numerous platinum discs. The problem was, singing about south-central and bling sounded ridiculous coming from a Brummie-Londoner. Okay, many pop artists might fake an Atlantic drawl for mainstream sales, but for a white kid from Birmingham to apparently aspire to sounding like a black gangsta rapper was disastrous: Run DMC, Ice Cube and Snoop Dogg have never been to Selly Oak. The teenage Skinner wasn't the first and he certainly was not to be the last to fall into this trap. He says his early demos sounded little more than copies of De La Soul and the Beastie Boys. Ali G might be the logical comic evolution of this phenomenon but Skinner would, fortunately, soon see the error of his ways.

Paradoxically, although Skinner was hypnotised by hip-hop, strangely enough he chose not to go down the sampling route: 'De La Soul's *3 Feet High And Rising* was a very important album for me when I was a kid. (But) as for sampling, I'd rather write the song,' he explained to the *CMJ* web magazine. 'That's not because I'm any better than them — it's just a part of my ego. I'd rather have people think that I made it ... rather than sample ... it earns you more money. However, the first track that I ever made had a sample of 'It's Not Unusual', by Tom Jones in it!'

He states that this first fully realised song was completed at the tender age of only fifteen. Once that had been completed, the floodgates opened and the scribbled observations from his little notebooks soon started evolving into song after song. An unlikely inspiration came in the form of Jimi Hendrix, not in the sense of his guitar genius or even his music, but in his dedication to perfection. Skinner read about Hendrix's obsessive rehearsing and writing streak and endeavoured to replicate that for his own music (suitably, he later name-checks Jimi on the opening track of his debut album, 'Turn The Page'). The results of such diligence were swift and fruitful. Using that wardrobe as a booth, splicing the beats together with his crude studio set-up and programming the music himself, Mike Skinner's music was about to take off.

At the age of 19, he travelled to Australia, like so many thousands of other teenagers, in cohorts with his then-girlfriend and apparently against the advice of all his family and friends. He worked various jobs during his time Down Under, including at a call centre, before the relationship splintered (she broke it off apparently), and he returned, more tanned, more experienced and possibly less enamoured with life outside Blighty. *The Guardian*'s Richard Jinman reported that a call centre colleague spoke of 'a confident, smartly dressed young man who was happy to share his plans for the music industry with anyone who would listen.'

Years later, he would tour the vast continent alongside the Beastie Boys and the Chemical Brothers and feature high on the bill of the annual spectacular, 'The Big Day Out' (where he would later do a live cover of the Beastie Boys' 'Fight For Your Right (To Party)'.

Back in London, where his family had moved for the latter part of his childhood, Skinner's burgeoning interest in music and prolific writing of material continued apace. Inevitably, he had given his project a name – The Streets. It is well-known that The Streets was originally a collaboration with Mike and various friends but over the years, the focus centred more and more on Mike. Years later, when asked what his strengths and weaknesses were, Skinner felt his quest for perfectionism was often a double-edged sword: 'I think (that's one of) my biggest faults and my biggest strengths, being a perfectionist. I can get some really good results by never being happy with what I'm doing at the time. I find it hard working with anyone else. I don't work well in a band.'

So for the purposes of releasing albums in the future, it was just him, just The Streets. Dictionary buffs might point out that the use of the definite article followed by a plural noun suggested there was more than one person in the band, but I've heard worse. Richard James calls himself Aphex Twin and he's not got a twin. The Game isn't a board game at all, he's a man formerly in G-Unit.

"Splicing the beats together with his crude studio set-up and programming the music himself, Mike Skinner's music was about to take off."

Knowing him as we do now, this is a classic Skinnerism, deflecting attention away from himself and hiding behind a façade that makes people think. As he told Ben Thompson in *The Observer*, 'I love the name 'The Streets', because it leaves so much to the imagination.'

CHAPTER 2:
UNDERNEATH
THE ARCHES

'What I'm trying to do [when I write songs] is reduce words and images and sounds down to the bone.'

Not Mike Skinner. Brian Ferry.

Mike Skinner has somehow emerged as an artist devoid of too much baggage from any 'scene', a stifling millstone that has seen many good bands suffocated and even more bad bands unnecessarily signed to a lucrative record deal. However, he did spill out from underneath a rock with several similar artists crawling under it, and that particular rock was garage.

There are obvious overtures to his background in the title of his debut album, *Original Pirate Material*. Pirate radio was not exclusive to garage, nor indeed was it particularly new. Oddly enough, it had its antecedents in the forefathers of Radio 1 – a mainstream monstrosity that latterday garage would openly mock and detest – in the shape of stations such as Radio Caroline and Radio Luxembourg.

Such unlicensed radio stations broadcast shows from just outside British territorial waters and therefore outside the jurisdiction of UK law (hence 'pirate', although some radios worked from disused naval forts on the Thames Estuary too). These radios enjoyed massive listening figures – the two market-leaders, Radio London and Radio Caroline, boasted figures of between six and eight million, stats that modern-day radio stations would give their right arm for. Then, suddenly, it all ended when Harold Wilson's Labour government introduced the Marine Broadcasting Offences Act in August 1967, effectively bringing in state powers to stop such broadcasts – if necessary, physically.

The BBC had spotted the demand nonetheless, and thus gave birth to Radio 1, poaching many former pirate pioneers such as Tony Blackburn, John Peel, Johnny Walker and Dave Lee Travis. True, the late, great John Peel maintained this cutting edge approach throughout his broadcasting life but other than that, with a few notable exceptions, the atmosphere of innovation soon merged into the banal playlists and broad appeal of mainstream broadcasting.

Of more immediacy for the late 90s garage scene was the early 80s popularity of pirate radio within black music, when stations such as Horizon, LWR and the brilliantly-titled Dread Broadcasting Corporation sent out signals from rather more terrestrial boltholes. Their popularity was such that the government even formed a branch of the Department of Trade and Industry known unofficially as 'anti-pirate agents'. It didn't work – technology allowed the transmitter's signal to be 'thrown' to far-flung locations and by the end of that decade of excess, there were said to be 600 stations regularly broadcasting.

> *"The BBC had spotted the demand nonetheless, and thus gave birth to Radio 1, poaching many former pirate pioneers."*

Draconian legislation at the turn of the new decade almost extinguished pirates altogether (Kiss was originally a pirate but after a government amnesty won a legitimate licence), but the rave scene and yet more home-grown technology (and mobile phones) fuelled another rebirth in around 1992 (for a while there was even hybrid rave-rap, with performers like Rebel MC, Ragga Twins, and Demon Boyz). The stalking ground for UK garage had been created.

The history of UK garage would fill a thousand pages but its relevance to the appearance of The Streets is entirely valid. Gradually, MCs had tired of their supporting role to DJs and now commanded – and demanded – equal billing. Generally, instead of one DJ, these crews would have many members. Pretty soon, the underground was flooded with key acts such as MC collectives like So Solid Crew, K2 Family, Pay As U Go Kartel, GK Allstars, Dem Lott, Horra Squad and Nasty Crew.

The music centred around the work of MCs, vocal samples and the rather clumsily-titled 'two-step', which reminded the listener of house, jungle, reggae, drum and bass, a snippet of R&B and yet none of the above. It is a complex beast best left to the experts to describe: James Huggett of *The Village Voice* details it thus: 'intricate percussion patterns, highly-textured drum sounds, and above all, the skippy, snappy, syncopated snares and busy, bustling hi-hats that make garage much more funky than regular house.'

London was the epicentre (although other cities such as Birmingham, Manchester etc would all lay claim to their own contribution). The scene centred somewhere between the railway arches of underground garage clubs and the illicit pirate radio stations. In the early 90s, garage producers/DJs such as Masters At Work, Nice & Ripe, Strictly Rhythm and Tuff Jam were earning a solid reputation that took their studio sounds into the edgier clubs of the capital. Most of the high street clubs/major club chains turned a cold shoulder to garage, but that merely sent it further underground and effectively gave it more credibility. Soon enough, the scene had spurned its own clubs such as The Park in Kensington, Cafe De Paris, The Gass Club, Twice As Nice at the Coliseum and The Fitness Centre. One of the most popular and notorious nights was at The Arches in London – from here came Radio 1's Dreem Teem for example.

The 'celebrity' element of this scene was not bands or singers, but MCs. Although at first, the key MCs shunned the spotlight, they inevitably became 'big names': pioneers such as MC Creed. People such as God's Gift from Pay As You Go or the MCs of Nasty Crew became as feted within their own ranks as any

MTV-friendly pop star, regardless of their mainstream success of not.

For those who couldn't get enough garage at the clubs or, increasingly, those who were too young to get in, there were the pirate radios running in tandem with these club nights. Notable stations were Freek, London Underground, Rinse, Déjà Vu, Rinse, Y2K, Shine and Raw Mission. Their illegal broadcasting frequencies became etched in the brains of the text-generation, beaming out tunes and mixes from a make-shift transmitter and a roomful of energy, ever-vigilant in the

"The scene centred somewhere between the railway arches of underground garage clubs and the illicit pirate radio stations."

face of police crack-downs. This was not a scene that was ever destined to find itself on *Richard & Judy*. For garage, the 1990s equivalent of a boat at sea was usually the roof of a council block, a disused flat, occasionally for the riskier few, a back-street, lock-up (among the penalties threatened by a worried establishment were two years' jail and confiscation of all equipment, even personal record collections).

The first missives from the garage trenches came in the form of songs such as Rosie Gaines' 'Closer Than Close' back in 1998. According to the definitive garage website, 'MC Pages' on ukflex.com, garage enjoyed its Number 1 with Shanks and Bigfoot's 'Sweet Like Chocolate'; the commerciality was cranked up another notch with MC Luck and DJ Neat's 'Little Bit of Luck',

which was both a massive garage tune and a chart hit.
Odd to think of it now, what with his cameo
appearances on Channel 4's surreal *Bo Selecta!* TV show,
but Craig David is a bastard child of UK garage. His
breakthrough track, courtesy of the Artful Dodger (later
referenced with a smirk by Skinner on 'Let's Push Things
Forward'), was 'Rewind' – now a phrase more associated
with a bear with an erection – was at the time was a
huge tune on the underground. Pushing the envelope
further still, the pop band Blazin' Squad originally
started off life as a ten-piece garage outfit apeing
So Solid Crew and quickly earned acclaim in the garage
media with their debut track, 'Standard Flow',
self-released on their own Weighty Plates label. To this
day, the remix of that tune with Elephant Man is still
played on dedicated garage radio shows. That act may
have taken the pop route and thus extinguished any
credibility they originally had in the garage scene, but
the fact is the genesis of that latterday chart-topping 'boy
band' was actually ten Essex/north London school kids
obsessed with MCs, DJs and straight-up garage.

They were not alone – kids all over the capital, and
in other parts of the country were buying decks, making
tapes, MC-ing at parties, battling with rival crews,
sampling, mixing, DJ-ing and living their lives for
garage. The scene became so popular with this
demograph that scores of under-18s nights sprouted up
to meet demand, at rather more innocuous venues such
as Epping Forest Country Club, whose Atlantis night
was a big success. And, as a notable exception to many
underground dance scenes, the girls' opinions were just
as important as the boys'. There was even an all-female
garage crew called Feminine Pressure.

Of course, the commercial zenith – or nadir, depending on your view – was when So Solid Crew's breath-taking '21 Seconds To Go' entered the UK singles chart at Number 1 in August 2001. *Top of the Pops*, long since the bastion of middle England's music knowledge, had never seen anything like it before. Thirty or more in the band, a video that made your skin crawl but fascinated at the same time, a song that was as addictive as it was dark, a breakthrough if ever there was one.

Apparently not. Inevitably, people do not always necessarily take a positive view of acts who stick their head above the parapet. For many, So Solid going to Number 1 was the moment UK garage lost its edge. Unfair, surely. Worse still, the hit single brought that pioneering band, and the scene from whence it came, to the cynical and prowling eye of a far more intimidating beast: the UK's press. The tabloid and broadsheet media had found their new pariah.

The Dreem Teem and Tuff Jam got their own shows on Kiss FM, the media started writing about this latest 'scene' and record labels began scouting for the new So Solid. However, the elements of violence in the scene gave the tabloids all the ammunition it needed. Although the garage scene shared many genealogical roots with the late 80s/early 90s rave scene, cocaine was the drug of choice, not ecstasy. The press also made mileage out of this so-called 'champagne-and-cocaine' mentality.

So Solid were the focus of the press bile; when there was a shooting at an Astoria gig in London's West End, venues started pulling gigs, strangely paralleling the experience of the establishment-baiting Sex Pistols way back in 1976-7. Except this time, the behemoth of the media was too mighty for one band or one scene to fight. Garage began to be pushed back underground.

It is easy to forget among all the hype and rhetoric that people such as Mega Man, Romeo, Wylie and Asher D were expert and quite brilliant MCs and rappers. It wasn't about individuals either. Along the way, various hybrids and cross-fertilisations occurred – for example when jungle spilled into the garage clubs around 1995 – which in turn created some of modern music's most specific and yet essential subgenres, like speed garage. MCs and DJs switched between the ranks of these closely-affiliated genres and a melting pot of talent and unorthodox music was fired up even more. In that pot was a Brummie-cum-Londoner by the name of Mike Skinner …

"Like many of his garage contemporaries, Skinner spent a long time obsessed with the Wu-Tang Clan."

By then, of course, Skinner wasn't just a hip-hop freak. You can't slither along the underground without picking up at least some of its creatures – thus hip-hop was partnered with garage, then Mike developed a taste for jungle and house music too. Spurred on by the DIY ethic of the garage scene – akin to punk's ethos – he tried to set up his own label to put out his music and that of his friends and fellow collaborators with whom he spent much of his waking hours. Much of the 2-step genre is 'home-made', using simple and easily available technology. Many wannabee producers use downloadable 'studio' programs widely available on the net or even

PlayStation's beat-making software.

Like many of his garage contemporaries, Skinner spent a long time obsessed with the Wu-Tang Clan. He makes no secret of his passion for the kung fu obsessions and dark content of that particular seminal rap act, even though in many ways it is a million miles from his own later work. As Gil Kaufman of *MTV News* astutely said in an interview with Mike in 2002, 'Replace Shaolin with ancient Roman warriors, Strong Island with grimy London pubs and the "n" word with "geezers" and you have The Streets.'

CHAPTER 3: STREETS BECOME HEROES

Sylvester Stallone – former lion cage cleaner

Mick Jagger – porter at a mental hospital

Rod Stewart – gravedigger

Ozzy Osbourne – slaughter house labourer

George Michael – Saturday boy at Bhs

Boy George – Tesco shelf-stacker

Madonna – former Dunkin' Donuts protégé

Mike Skinner – former Burger King 'team member'

The Holloway Road is famous for several things. There's a really cheap bathroom 'centre' halfway up. On the other side, further south, there's a weird shop selling all sorts of reptiles, snakes, fish and assorted menagerie. It's also where one of the earliest super-producers, Joe Meek, the man behind mega-selling song 'Telstar', shot his landlady then killed himself on the eighth anniversary of Buddy Holly's death (whom Meek claimed to have contacted in séances). Oh, and it's where Nick Worthington used to run a record shop. Not Nick Hornby, Nick Worthington.

Worthington ran a (then) relatively small-scale record label from the shop, using the name Locked On. It was to this modest office that a young Mike Skinner brought a tape of his tunes. It wasn't just the tape he talked about either. He knew what was going to be on 'his first album' too, as Worthington explained to Richard Jinman of *The Guardian*: 'Normally when people say things like that, it's "yeah right", but he really did have it all worked out. The music just grabbed you because it was honest and real. He was just talking about his life which meant it sounded sincere and genuine.'

Locked On established itself as a genuine street-worthy label producing some of the most innovative speed garage and 2-step tracks around. Among the notable products of that label were well-respected club tracks from Tuff Jam, the Artful Dodger featuring Craig David, Dem 2, and Doolally. Funnily enough, although Skinner was a fan of garage, he was always something of an outsider, making his tapes and tunes alone, skirting around the fringes of the scene and only dipping into its murky waters on occasion. An observer, more than a player, if you like. Later, when he was scouring around the USA on his first promotional tour over there, Skinner even seemed to distance himself a little from the garage cognoscenti at the centre of the scene: 'There's the So Solid Crew. But really I'm the only one doing it this way.'

On the tape that landed on Worthington's desk was a track called 'Has It Come To This?'. Worthington was startled by the tape's brilliance, got in touch with a quiet and clearly pleased Skinner, and within a few short weeks, put out this track as The Street's debut single.

No wonder Worthington was impressed.

Skinner had been writing ... constantly. One of his favourite methods of capturing whatever his muse produced was to text himself on his mobile phone (a Motorola and, no, he isn't sponsored by them) – with his now-indispensable iPod, he has all the musical references he needs at his fingertips. Skinner is a voracious reader, often poring over classic novels, at other times reading manuals on script-writing. His taste in music is equally eclectic. Teddy Hanson, one his future cohorts from an act called the Mitchell Brothers says, 'He likes Johnny Cash and everything from ragga to rock ... What I like about his kind of music is that it sounds like he's really thought about it.' Mike's writing was often captured in his bedroom at his mom's house.

In his bedroom. That old chestnut. Daniel Bedingfield did it, The Prodigy's Liam Howlett did it. Skinner wasn't the first but no matter how many times you hear of this tale, you can't help but wonder at some pasty kid with his curtains drawn, making music on his own that is about to blow the music industry apart (well, the last two did anyway). Living with his mother also made it financially viable for Mike to spend so much time on his music – otherwise he would have had to get a building site job. At one point during the final phase of what would become his debut album, he took to office work at Marks & Spencer, surrounded by lingerie;

there were other menial jobs such as working at a petrol station, but essentially The Streets was the only job that mattered.

Few saw it coming. Veteran journalist Ted Kessler of *NME* did. Knowing what we do now, it is easy to listen to that track and say we would have spotted it too. We didn't; he did. Take his prophetic review of 'Has It Come To This?' "It sounds like a very bad idea: a 22-year-old white Brummie called Mike rapping over his own home-made garage under the nom de plume of The Streets. The 2 Step Brian Harvey, has it really come to this? But 'Has It Come To This?' is not only the most original, lyrical British rap in memory, it also (alongside So Solid Crew) charts an evolutionary route for UK garage. 'Has It Come To This?' is the first garage record to be made about those who buy the records, rather than about those who make them.

It is not about being bling bling or VIP in Napa. It is about getting stoned playing Playstation, about scoring drugs, about being menaced in kebab shops, about hanging round on corners looking for better, about new trainers and breaking windows ... A major talent has arrived ..."

... But not in the Top Ten. Considering Skinner's later lofty status and apparent critical invincibility, his first four singles – everything released off his debut album, basically – did not pierce the Top Ten. Indeed, only the first single, 'Has It Come To This?' breached the Twenty (the following three hitting 30, 27 and 21 respectively – more to follow).

Where were we in October 2001? Well, Kylie Minogue had finally re-launched a career that had stalled several times, finally hitting Number 1 with the classic 'Can't Get You Out Of My Head'. Dido's album *No Angel* sold 2.4 million copies in the UK alone that year; Craig David became the youngest male ever to write and sing a chart-topper with 'Fill Me In'; Hear'Say became the first of a generation of TV audition show bands sent to the slaughter; Eminem performed with Elton John at the Grammys and Coldplay started to realise their ambition to be one of the world's biggest bands.

"It sounds like a very bad idea: a 22-year-old white Brummie called Mike rapping over his own home-made garage under the nom de plume of The Streets. The 2 Step Brian Harvey, has it really come to this?"

Of course, none of that actually mattered after 9/11.

With the smoke still seeping heavenwards and bodies still being pulled out of the wreckage of the Twin Towers, the context of Skinner's debut single seemed totally irrelevant. Like the rest of the charts.

But, nonetheless, Skinner had released his debut and a start had been made. Perhaps surprisingly, The Streets chose to release no further singles from the forthcoming debut album before that long player's February 2002 release. It was a risky policy, not having given the public chance to hear more snippets and thus begin to anticipate the album. It mattered not — when his first album *Original Pirate Material* was released in February of 2002, it hit an impressive Number 10 in the album charts. Best-seller.

On the surface that seems like a great start. Yet Skinner's debut album did not arrive in a fanfare of marketing budgets and TV adverts, nor did it come anywhere near an Asda 'Album of the Week' rack (not for now, anyway). It was quality word-of-mouth that did it. For a while.

I wasn't as sharp as Ted Kessler. I didn't see it coming, but then, few did. I'd read about a band called The

> *"In conversation, Skinner is relatively quietly-spoken, quite the opposite of the lairy, loud and in-yer-face delivery on many of his songs."*

Streets but not took too much notice; after all, there's only so many pronouncements of 'this is the next biggest thing' you can take seriously (Gay Dad?)

Then I bought the record and all hell broke loose.

It all starts with a track that, to this day, still sends shivers up my spine. 'Turn The Page'. The opening words of the album pounce out at you in Skinner's inimitable voice, over an instant volley of staccato strings blended seamlessly with a hypnotic beat. You know within twenty seconds that something is coming out of your stereo that you haven't heard before. Fifty years after rock and roll ripped up seats in cinemas and town halls nationwide, that is some realisation.

Immediately, you are pulled into this world that is a

curious mix of the gladiator and the hooligan. Both fighting for spectacle in front of their peers, one breed forced to, the other of their own volition. His choice of scenario is stark. At once Skinner takes you into a coliseum, then back to a railway arch, skips over to a garage battle, effortlessly. The Bullring is mentioned. We know this man is bastard child of garage, we hear of spitting lyrics, his crew, cheap rhymes. We have so many Skinnerisms, so many lyrical staples of his forthcoming body of work. Geezers, birds, warriors. There is an ambiguous reference to garage burning down, a Biblical snippet with fires raging for forty days, jungle makes an appearance as do shopping malls. Another staple is how raw and simple it all is. That one stabbing string phrase, repeated over and over, the bass barely moving, simple, effective, startling.

Perhaps most striking – and arguably Skinner's single greatest strength on record – is the absolute clarity of his diction. In conversation, Skinner is relatively quietly-spoken, quite the opposite of the lairy, loud and in-yer-face delivery on many of his songs. Yet somehow the words that spill out of the speaker are as clear, audible and understandable as if Skinner was sitting next to you in a library and whispering untold stories in your ear. Tales of horror, of men felled by vindictive blows, blood-thirsty on-lookers snarling their appreciation, a family tree of violence and broken bones, traced back centuries and yet bang up to date, current, harrowing, real. With such vocal clarity, it is impossible not to get drawn into his world.

You cannot underestimate the power of that opening track. I can pretend to be cool and well-informed, above being impressed, but the fact is, when I first heard 'Turn

The Page', my view of music changed forever. Skinner might fidget uncomfortably if he reads that, but there you go. I am not ashamed. Apparently, if you listen really closely, you can hear his mother telling him to 'turn the music down, it's dinner time'. I can't, maybe I have got too much wax in there. Listening to 'Turn The Page' at maximum volume and on repeat, it is like hearing music for the first time, wax or no wax. In the song he says he is miles ahead and being chased ... only these few short minutes into *Original Pirate Material* and that statement is undeniable.

After such a start, the perky garage beats and tinkling jazzy keyboard signature of debut single 'Has It Come To This?' provide welcome respite, musically at least. The subject matter is still ultra-gritty though. We also meet our first collaborator, with Calvin Schmalvin's soulful vocals slinking its way through the title line. The lyrical pace is breathless again, making you feel like you've been reading a book for a week when you are only on track two. In a multi-media world obsessed with 'content', Skinner doesn't come up short.

Unusually perhaps, Mike chooses to name-drop himself or rather his band name, a brief nod to the self-referential obsession of the more indulgent and egotistical edges of his beloved hip-hop. Name-dropper and self-publicist he may not be, but some felt that Skinner's supposedly 'humble' hip-hop was little more than the usual ego-driven indulgence in another guise. In reply to accusations that he was every bit as egotistical as the more obvious strutting peacocks of hip-hop – on the basis that all he did was write and sing about himself – Skinner was dismissive: 'If you're telling a story, you have to tell it from your perspective. That's just the way

I'm telling my stories. It's not like, "Hey, look at me. I'm great."'

There are brazen mentions of pirate radio, drugs and urban deprivation. Two tracks in and it is already apparent that Skinner has made sure you've missed the last bus home and it's just you and his seedy, insular, dank world for company. Said to be what Skinner thinks one of his heroes, DJ Premier, would sound like if he had been born a garage head, this song ramps up the stakes another notch.

Although Skinner has denied too much overt influence from the Two Tone scene in the late 70s, The Specials lie heavily all over the third track on *OPM*, namely 'Let's Push Things Forward'. More garage, more lyrical excellence, more musical cross-breeding. Listening to the doleful brass line that runs through the song like a spine of ska infection, you can almost see the car-full of Specials, Jerry Dammers toothless grin in the back, Terry Hall's striking melancholic face in the front, driving through the monochrome landscapes of the 'Ghost Town' video almost twenty five years earlier.

Back then, of course, Britain's socially disadvantaged and economically weaker population were having the life throttled out of them by Thatcher. 'Ghost Town' was that fizzing moment when a song from the underground perfectly captured the sense of discontent and disenfranchisement that riddled the millions in the snaking unemployment queue and beyond. Maybe Skinner's referencing the riots with his mention of Brixton burning up, maybe not. His politics are at their most effective when he is being apolitical.

Besides, 'Let's Push Things Forward' is more concerned with the politics of music than that of

Westminster. The thrust of the chorus is how creatively bankrupt so much of music is and how certain acts, The Streets included, are in the minority trying to push the boundaries. You wonder how much of hip-hop Skinner is including in his list of musical disappointment, pointing out the irrelevance of the word 'bitch' in his own street culture. Chastising those who moan about sterility in music but then purchase regardless, the song is a confident man at work – after all, people in glass houses and all that.

After running at such a level for three songs in a row, it was understandable that there might soon be a dip. It comes with 'Sharp Darts', a blatant battle boast, setting out Skinner's stall as welcoming all-comers to compete against him in the railway arches, but giving them scant chance of a victory. The problem is that a rattling snare beat and plodding bass don't quite work on the same exquisite level as the beats earlier in the album. Heavy hip-hop it may be, but the impact is relatively lightweight. Lyrically, of course, Skinner is deft, adventurous and complex, but the edge of conceit that is utterly necessary for someone to win a battle in front of expectant garage freaks somehow detracts from Skinner's previous originality. This is *8 Mile* for the garage generation, polished, intriguing but not as essential as material elsewhere on the record.

'Same Old Thing' is the first time we plunge head first, arms tied, into the world of pubs, booze, fights and excess that Mike's lyrics would soon be famous for. The ominous strings take us this time somewhere between an odd 60s sci-fi monster moment, and some Hitchcock classic. You listen and feel glad that you aren't caught up in whatever chaos is about to explode ... although you still want to see what happens. Football, birds, booze, it should read like a clichéd list of some out-of-print lads mag, but somehow Skinner pulls it off. It works.

If parts of 'Same Old Thing' were unsettling, all of 'Geezers Need Excitement' is downright frightening. Bouyed by escorting us into his local drinking hole on the previous track, Skinner drags us to the nearby takeaway for some unnecessary and frantic scrapping. More strings soundtrack the clever beats with a veneer of class that belies the violent and brutal scenario being recounted. This track could easily have supplanted itself on Skinner's second album, but sitting here as a stand-alone track, it is no less potent. The influence of Wu-Tang Clan, certainly in the atmosphere and also to a degree in the music, is clear.

There is a certain black comedy to the fight that erupts over chips being thrown, over owing your dealer money and over his drunken infidelities, but this is no laugh-a-minute comedy store. Although he sneakily references *Lock, Stock and Two Smoking Barrels* and the ensuing gangster-chic movie/soundtrack/ fashion that proved so popular in a thousand cinema lobbies across the country, Skinner makes no secret that away from the pop corn and upholstered, Pepsi-spattered seats, this existence is not a lifestyle of comfort. He peels back the lid for us to peak inside from a safe distance, and all we see is cold violence.

The Streets' first 'ballad' is up next, 'It's Too Late'. The debut album's sister track to 'Dry Your Eyes'. It's a good job that Skinner knows his sampling techniques and strings programming, otherwise he would have had the world's biggest invoice from the Royal Philharmonic. But the strings never tire, they just become one of his traits, one of the elements of the album you expect and enjoy. The subject matter surprises, coming so soon after the bravado of the street-fighting years of 'Geezers Need Excitement'. Skinner is dumped, Skinner is gutted, Skinner knows he deserves it and Skinner knows there is nothing he can do to redeem himself. It's all bluntly honest, from the obvious heartache he feels, through the rain falling on his face (hiding a tear perhaps?), to the fact that he still adores his former girlfriend. In one song Mike distances himself from the more macho commercial fringes of hip-hop forever. You realise there is much more to this Fred Perry-wearing geezer who was, only a few hours ago, smashing someone's head off a fast food shop floor. The plot thickens.

Then, as if to reassert his masculinity, Mike sends us straight into an all-out, pissed up night of pure, unadulterated debauchery that is 'Too Much Brandy'. Mushrooms, too much drinking, dark alleys, cocaine, paranoia, it's all in there. 'There's frustration and you want to prove yourself,' he told one magazine, 'but I don't think it could be any other way, really. It's more about the biology of the age. You got all these hormones and your head's all over the place compared to when you were growing up. Adults used to say, "Yeah, it's really crazy when you're a teenager." I thought, "Well, I don't feel that crazy. It's when you get older that it's pretty crazy."'

The musical backdrop is like some odd theme tune from a 70s kids cartoon, although the subject of excess is far from child-like. This is an unreservedly adults-only experience. By the time the characters in the song are stumbling along a late night, dimly-lit street towards a much-needed pillow and drunken slumber, you could almost be forgiven for forgetting that moment of weakness on the previous track.

Talking of drink, 'Don't Mug Yourself' was written while drunk, according to Skinner. It was also, as will be discussed later, written with the shadow of Eminem over his shoulder. There is certainly an element of that comic-book comedy and bravado that Slim Shady best shows us on tracks like 'The Real Slim Shady', but this is about as 'American-rap' as an iced bun. Yet somehow, the comic sound of the track adds to the flavour of what the miscreants in the tale are up to. Skinner cleverly

"He peels back the lid for us to peak inside from a safe distance, and all we see is cold violence."

reinforces the kitchen-sink scenarios with a greasy spoon, full English breakfasts and such like. It also introduces the most blatant injection of virtual-spoken-word into the album, with much of the lyrical content little more than a conversation to music. His mate Calvin tries his best to pull Skinner's character from embarrassing himself by being too openly keen on this mystery girl, but his pleas fall on deaf ears. The final crude free-styling of Calvin-Schmalvin cleverly gives us a fly-on-the-wall TV snippet of life inside Skinner's recording studio-cum-bedroom.

Ramming the increasingly narrative-focussed album back to a dance beat, the tenth track 'Who Got The Funk?' is indeed just a groove. The funk guitar and wah-

wah effects, complete with 70s diva-like female backing vocals, rounded off with snappy horn blasts, make this Skinner's most overtly dance-influenced tune. Working his way round his most popular haunts and geezers, Skinner self-references again, but the neat throwback to 'Has It Come To This?' seems entirely fitting. He keeps it brief, and it works beautifully.

Just when you think he has settled back to some good, unashamed beats, Skinner drags us back into a dark comedy on Channel 4, with the pure narrative dialogue of 'The Irony Of It All'. Reminding the listener of the students-cum-dealers and the hard-as-nails street

"In the world that Skinner's debut album resides in, the weak do not generally become heroes."

louts in the aforementioned *Lock, Stock* … film, the song details a collision of two worlds: the boozed-up, bullish hooligan Terry, whose favourite phrase would undoubtedly be 'wot you lookin' at?'; versus the self-righteous, informed but painfully twee weed-smoking student Tim. When the vegetarian, pot-smoking, Gail Porter-loving, Playstation-obsessed student talks, the jaunty piano accompaniment mixes music hall with *Carry On*, then it smashes straight back into a far more ominous string-laden, almost military-like overture for 'law-abiding' Terry. This is like the best episode of *Trisha* ever broadcast. It's hard to see this song as anything other than a comedy sketch. Frightening at times, but comic nonetheless.

In the world that Skinner's debut album resides in, the weak do not generally become heroes. They normally get beaten shitless. Nonetheless, this does not stop the twelfth track being one of the many highlights of this record. Yet more wistful strings are laid over one of the record's softest beats, contrasted by Skinner's vocal being the highest in the mix so far. Soulful rhythms abound, even though he is still talking about ecstasy and being horny. Suitably loved up, the emotions take over and violence is forgotten, imagining the world's leaders on happy drugs (who says they aren't?). Having bottomed out when he was dumped, and scraped the barrel fighting in the fast food shop, Skinner's lead player here is enjoying his drugs, his night out and his life. He would later counter claims that he is a bad role model by strongly denying he countenances drug abuse, rather than use: 'We all need to escape sometimes. But there's this myth that when you talk about taking drugs, you're talking about becoming a drug addict and that isn't what I suggest.'

For once blatantly political, Skinner name-checks the DJs who have meant something to him during his life, before flipping the bird to the government and its Criminal Justice Bill. This brief political spat seems oddly out of place, but for a talent spewed forth from one of the most demonised musical genres of recent years, it is an indulgence he should perhaps be allowed. It is said to be about his first experience of 'E', but it is hard not to see the song as some sort of sentimental history of the rave culture. One admiring writer said this was 'the best, most honest song about E culture since Pulp's 'Sorted for E's and Wizz'. Who is to disagree?

Unlucky thirteen was the track 'Who Dares Wins' and,

to be honest, it's the only unlucky track for the listener. It sounds like a tribute act to The Streets, a poor imitation, even though we've only known him at this stage for one single and twelve album tracks. Fortunately, it's all over before it's begun, so let's move on.

Closing the album is 'Stay Positive', vocally delivered not by Skinner but by one of his cohorts in the game. As dark in tone as the album that it concludes, the lyrics are as sharp as ever, talking of more draw, more rain, more grim inner city mundanity, smack, and so on. Faced with this litany of depressing obstacles, the positivity which Skinner dangles in the face like a fresh carrot is hard to grasp. To be fair, set against the preceding tracks sung/delivered by Mike Skinner, the vocalist does a sterling job of finishing the album. If ever this was a brief to fuck up, this was it, but he does the job with aplomb. And one of the last instruments you hear on the record that many say redefined dance, garage, hip-hop and pretty much every other street music you care to whisper? A harp. Beat that.

... and then it is over. You feel like you need to put the kettle on ... well, I did anyway. You almost want to rewind the video tape and pick out the best bits, until you remember it wasn't a film. Short of transplanting a projector inside your brain, Mike Skinner couldn't have delivered a more visual debut album. Despite its complexities, lyrical verbosity and musical split personalities, *Original Pirate Material* was somehow instantly as addictive as the crack that it warns you off within. Problem was, one fix was not enough. Press repeat.

Although this album was never sold as, or purported to be, a concept album, Skinner's monotone, hypnotic voice is so prevalent and mixed so upfront that it is hard to think of the vignettes he paints as anything other than at least semi-autobiographical and somehow connected, however thinly.

The urban myth that he recorded it in his bedroom is absolutely true, as I have said. Generous estimates predict it cost him no more than £4,000. To put that in context, that would buy you about twenty minutes with a super-producer or alternatively less than a day's recording at a top London studio. The word 'recoup' was clearly not necessary in Skinner's vocabulary.

"Mike Skinner had almost made a generation of acts obsolete overnight."

Not only did *Original Pirate Material* quantify so many previous records as under-achieving, it also set new parameters for what came after. You could almost hear some of his peers, deep in the final mix of their new album, pressing delete and starting again when they heard what he had produced. *Original Pirate Material* raised the stakes for *everyone*. That is no cheap hyperbole, just a simple statement of fact.

Via razor sharp wit, killer beats ranging from hip-hop to house and from jungle to soul, exquisite sample selection and usage, a disturbing ability to absolutely nail the grim reality of so much of British life with a sprinkling of words and the confidence to make his first impression with an album that was like nothing that had gone before, Mike Skinner had almost made a generation of acts obsolete overnight. If it was my own group competing with this, unless I was drenched in self-belief I would have packed up there and then, sold my decks and slunk off unnoticed. Call me a quitter but I would know when I was beaten. Stay down.

CHAPTER 4:
NO CHILLI SAUCE PLEASE

'I've become a bit disillusioned with kebabs, because they put a whole load of lettuce and onions and stuff in the pita bread and they put the meat on the top and the sauce on that. When you bite into it, you get a whole load of meat and sauce in the first bite, then after that you've just got a bread and lettuce sandwich.' Mike Skinner, again.

What did the press think of *Original Pirate Material*? Where do you want to start? How about this from *The Observer*: 'a superbly fresh and witty distillation of what it felt like to be young and

British at the start of a new century. This record also performs a unique balancing act, somehow managing to be both the next step forward for the great domestic pop songwriting tradition which stretched back from Massive Attack's *Blue Lines* to Madness and the Specials, to the Kinks and the Who, and a disc with the power to unite the disparate tribes of UK dance music – the ravers, hip-hop heads, garagistas – in the volatile camaraderie of the late-night kebab queue.'

Or how about this:'(It's) all changed since the arrival of The Streets' *Original Pirate Material*, a record that does for British rhyming what William Shakespeare did for London theatre – gives it a Nike-shoed kick in the ass.'

The Daily Mirror called it 'one of the best British debut albums of the past twenty years'; *The Independent on Sunday* said it was 'one of the most important albums of 2002. Genius is not too strong a word'; and *NME* said 'the future of dance music *is* The Streets'. Elsewhere, the album was compared to the Clash's debut mixed with *Trainspotting*, ... and so on and so on.

Basically, I could fill this book with rave reviews of Mike Skinner's debut album. His press file for the record is more of a vast archive than a folder. Finding a bad review is like looking for something tasty in a nut roast. It just isn't there.

Mike was taken aback by the rave acclaim, but having so recently been frustrated and even by his own admission 'angry at obsessively making music and no one ever taking any notice', it was all very welcome. Naturally, he also had his own opinion as to why the praise was quite so fervent:'I think it's honest, bold, and quite courageous. Although it's not like I sat down and said to myself, "I'm going to make a really great, bold album." All I did was make an album that was as honest as I could make it. I never thought it would do what it has done. It's just so different that it could have easily crashed and burned.'

While a thousand earnest guitar bands claim that all they want to do is play music in their bed-sits and the money, fame, women and drugs are just something they have to, er, cope with, Skinner made no secret of the fact that he wanted success, but didn't expect it. 'I knew I was doing something no one else had ever done, and I knew people would respect it. I never thought it would sell.

"Finding a bad review is like looking for something tasty in a nut roast. It just isn't there."

No one ever thought it would sell. Even the people who bought it never thought it would sell.'

The gong-givers quickly followed the public's lead. *Original Pirate Material* was nominated for no less than four Brit Awards namely, 'Best Album', 'Best Urban Act', 'Best Breakthrough Artist', and 'Best British Male'. Maybe Skinner had been tipped off about the forthcoming 'award duck' so he didn't attend the ceremony at all, at which he won precisely no awards whatsoever.

He was also nominated for the more prestigious albeit commercially less empowering Mercury Award. The early signs were good for Mike, with the Mercury Prize jury chairman, Simon Frith, publicly praising The

Streets' album and work: 'The critics' favourite, the industry's favourite and the bookies' favourite; I think this is a very remarkable record from a teenage young man talking about what it's like to be young in the city.'

The Mercury Prize has distinguished itself over the years for often going with the underdog – recall the surprise when Roni Size won and the public and media alike were sent scurrying to the record shop to actually find out who he was. Unfortunately for Mike on this occasion, the more commercially palatable Ms Dynamite won, although that is not to dilute her brilliant single 'It Takes More' (and the corresponding album *A Little Deeper*), which ironically similarly ridiculed the bling-bling culture and rampant sexism of so much of hip-hop's more mutated commercial fringes. So Skinner may have had an ally in the reality stakes, but it was Dynamite who took home the gong. Funny enough, after that moment, their careers have taken decidedly different paths, partly due to Dynamite's admirable decision to spend time with her first born child at home.

Mike did win some awards though, it wasn't all nominations. At the prestigious Ivor Novello Awards, Skinner won 'Best Contemporary Song' for 'Weak Become Heroes'. And when the music media drew up their end of year 'Best Of …' lists, Skinner's name was on the tip of everyone's tongue. *The Observer* went even further and made it Number 75 of the greatest British albums of *all-time*. Across the pond in the US, surprisingly, acclaim was similar. *Rolling Stone* called it the #1 debut album of the year; *The New York Times* named it the #5 album of the year; *USA Today* ranked it #3 album of the year; *Blender*, *Spin* and the *L.A. Times* called it one of the top albums of the year.

With hefty sales of his album (eventually topping the unbelievable one million mark) and a press file quickly filling his, er, garage, Mike Skinner's chances of any decent time-off were slimming by the minute. It was a busy summer in 2003 for Mike, with numerous festival appearances including slots in the middle of bills at Homelands, Glastonbury, T In The Park and the Reading and Leeds festivals. It was at the latter that Mike was very shocked to hear that audience sing back virtually all the words to his songs – something he would very soon have to get used to.

And the singles ... they just kept on coming. Next up was 'Let's Push Things Forward' in April of 2002, a few weeks after the album had been unleashed on the public. It came complete with an excellent video showing Skinner walking down the very streets that he so manages to capture in his lyrics – this, however, slumped at Number 30, a disappointment after the Top Twenty of the first single. For many a boy band or manufactured pop act, this drop of twelve places would have signalled the arrival of a swift, sharpened guillotine, but Locked On Records were far smarter than that. They knew what they had in their midst and they were not about to strangle it at birth.

Third up was the sentimental 'Weak Become Heroes' which was backed by remixes from X-Press 2's Ashley Beedle and Black Science Orchestra. Skinner was making a habit of using such names to work with on remixes and it certainly added an intriguing edge to his back-catalogue. Amazingly, on reflection, this single only managed to improve by three places on its predecessor single. Failing to puncture the Top Twenty on two out of three occasions was hardly the stuff of music legend, rather music obscurity, but Skinner was not to be deterred. He knew what we all know now. The album was out there, infecting the public, converting the heathens, slaying the opposition. It was only a matter of time, surely?

Finally, eight months after *Original Pirate Material* was released, The Streets put out their final single from the project, namely 'Don't Mug Yourself'. Mike was rewarded with his second-best chart placing so far, but

"As Skinner shuffled fairly shambolically through an awkward and rather stunted rendition, you could almost hear the knives of the garage fashionistas being sharpened. "

still outside the Top Twenty at 21. However, on a positive note, 'Don't Mug Yourself' earned him a vaunted appearance on the aunty-pleasing *Top of the Pops*. As Skinner shuffled fairly shambolically through an awkward and rather stunted rendition, you could almost hear the knives of the garage fashionistas being sharpened.

Skinner has said in the past that the only people he craves respect from are these garage heads who still live in the scene that he grew up in. His multitude of influences are well-documented, but it is these original pirate materialists whom he aspires to impress: 'From day one I've always been a garage head. They're the people that I most want to get respect from. The garage boys can be pretty conservative, but the scene is everything to me.'

Once again he drew from a very real life experience for this song's inspiration. Having hit a writer's block on the track, Skinner decided to call his mate Calvin and go to the cinema to watch *Monsoon Wedding*, a drama about Indian weddings and family life. Calvin arrived complete with a fat bottle of rum which only halfway through the laborious film, was empty. Mike and Calvin saw the film out through bleary eyes and went home to continue with more drinks. Encouraged by his night out, Skinner played Calvin the instrumental version of the song he was stuck on. 'I want to be on that!' shouted his friend, ignoring the fact he was not a singer. Skinner thought it was a, er, rum idea and hence we were blessed with 'Don't Mug Yourself'. A lyrical departure of sorts, at least for the first album, concerning the obsession with a girlfriend and the humiliation of unrequited love (it was also a tasty precursor to Mike's second album). Mike was so pleased with the unexpected collaboration, that he insisted it was inserted as a last-minute addition to his forthcoming album. 'It's the lairiest one on the album. It's got a lot more "Fuck you!" attitude in it. I daresay people will think its more poppy, but I don't want to turn into kiddy fodder.'

It wasn't all positive though. In February, 2003, the media reported 'a former songwriting friend, Shaun Kelly, claimed he helped pen some of the band's hits.' This allegedly included certain lyrics which had been used, such as from 'Has It Come To This?' Kelly had written and performed material with The Streets in 1998 and according to NME.com, the claim was that 'some tracks on the album *Original Pirate Material* sound remarkably similar to songs they wrote together.' He said in *The Sun* that 'I feel gutted and betrayed by someone I had trusted and considered a mate … Whenever I hear a Streets ' track on the radio or see Mike on TV, I can't help thinking that it could have been my success story, too.' The response from The Streets' camp was very short, refuting the claim and saying Shaun was 'just bitter.'

> ## "The considerable impact of Mike Skinner's debut album was, essentially, completely against the odds."

Later, with the debut album still fizzing in the charts, Skinner also released another on-line record, this time a 45 minute mix album. The track-listing was effectively a trawl through the records and artists that have meant something to Mike over the years and provided a very revealing insight into his *modus operandi*. Thus we have DMX sitting next to Busta Rhymes, as well as the not-surprising appearance of Wu-Tang Clan, Method Man and Redmann. But there were also more obscure/underground tracks too, such as DJ Faz and Mr Vegas.

Overall, the campaign for *Original Pirate Material* was a huge success, a slow-burner, yes, but eventually a triumph. Released on a small independent, born out of a villianised garage scene and standing at odds to the all-conquering hip-hop music that ruled the charts all over the world, the considerable impact of Mike Skinner's debut album was, essentially, completely against the odds.

CHAPTER 5:
SLIM SHANDY

'I'm a fairly with-it person, but this stuff is curling my hair.'
Tipper Gore, American campaigner against obscenities in rock music, speaking in the 80s. Not Mike Skinner.

Never one to sidestep a question, Mike Skinner was openly frank when questioned about the rarefied atmosphere and temptations that followed the raging success of his debut album. At first, he went back underground, earning himself the nom de plume of 'The Howard Hughes of UK garage', yet rather than hide behind this suitably colourful comparison, Skinner revealed to *The Observer* that it wasn't all so cosy and eccentric. 'To be honest, I did go a bit George Best for a while ... I just didn't do it where everyone else tends to do it. You see papers and magazines full of celebrities falling out of bars pissed, and you think "oh, that's terrible – all the photographers taking pictures of them", but then you realise if they didn't want that to happen they wouldn't have gone to the bars where all the photographers hang out ... I fall out of [my local] bar fucking every week and no one knows about it.'

This was a particularly startling revelation when you consider that Mike Skinner is an epileptic. Likewise his thinly veiled autobiographical accounts of drug-taking scattered across his body of work, like so many pills on a cheap, grubby carpet. It wasn't until 'Get Out Of My

> *"This was a particularly startling revelation when you consider that Mike Skinner is an epileptic."*

House' on his second album that this is mentioned, but on first hearing the character talking of his medication, the listener is not sure if he is joking to get at his girl. But it transpires he isn't. Nor is Skinner.

He had his first fit when he was only seven and during his pre-teen and early teenage years he was quite severely affected. Given that these are the most formative years of your life in many ways, this was no small disadvantage. Yet, ever the optimist, Skinner drew on that and now says it actually contributed to where he is today: 'I think it is one of the reasons why I'm so focused,' he told *The Observer's* Ben Thompson (in what is possibly the most insightful article yet written on Skinner) 'as it forced me to be less social throughout the period when my mates didn't know what they were doing. Music is kind of like my best friend – it's probably the reason I didn't go mad when I was a teenager, and it's probably been the one constant since things have kicked off.'

Tiredness, not drugs, are what he says is his condition's worst enemy. Like so many fellow sufferers, tube televisions are also contraband. Hence Skinner's house is filled with the less harmful flat-screen technology. As he has grown older, he has learnt to control the condition and can now go for years between fits – in 2004 he hadn't suffered one for four years.

"Tiredness, not drugs, are what he says is his condition's worst enemy."

In between the first and second album, The Streets buoyed his US fans by releasing a mini-album called *We All Got Our Runnins* in October 2003. Essentially a compilation of B-sides and remixes, the record was only available on-line. Although tracks such as 'Give Me Back My Lighter' are interesting enough, it was always going to be an interesting addition for the real fan, rather than a substantial new addition to Skinner's canon. There were intriguing remixes courtesy of underground stars such as Mr. Figit, Ashley Beedle and High Contrast, which reinforced Skinner's reputation for still having his ear to the ground. But this was always going to be little more than a taster for the forthcoming second album.

Whenever Mike Skinner opines on a subject, people listen. When that subject is music, people stop in their tracks. His favourite lyricists? 50 Cent? Eminem? Dre? No, Kenny Rogers and Johnny Cash. Skinner says that although the inspiration for his beats and rhythms come from hip-hop in the first instance, the wordsmiths coming out of the southern states focus his lyrical slant. Country has always been a genre that tends towards the ultra-real (and often depressing), frequently loading their songs with the exact same betrayals as in The Streets' material. Except without the kebabs.

Skinner has mentioned specific songs in the past such as Kenny Rogers' 'The Gambler', Dave Loggins' 'Please Come to Boston' and Harry Chapin's 'Sniper'. Strangely, though, Mike draws little from the music itself – perhaps a relief to his record company – saying country has 'got the worst rhythm.'

His views on hip-hop are equally enlightening. 'Hip-hop,' he explained to Ben Thompson, 'draws on different principles to other music. It's not purely sonic pleasure: it's conflict and action and story. It's the old way of making records – which is rhythm and noise – combined with a little bit of The A-Team, and that's exactly what I love about it ... 'However, like Ms Dynamite alongside him, he has reservations about the superstar former ghetto rappers who dominate so much of music television. 'When you listen to 50 Cent, you're hearing a guy who you imagine goes around getting shot, and he doesn't, really – well, he did, but now he's doing pretty much the same as I am: being interviewed, collecting awards, going to parties.' This celebrity lifestyle unavoidably extricates the rapper, says Skinner, from the very environment that provided the material for their breakthrough music. Which is fair comment and is certainly visible with some of the most high profile rappers – by 2005, even the notoriously creative Eminem appeared to be struggling for material that isn't about stardom or celebrity. To play devil's advocate for a moment, in early March 2005, one of 50 Cent's entourage was shot in the leg while the rapper was actually on air at a famous hip-hop radio station, so perhaps the multi-platinum discs and *Billboard* chart-toppers haven't quite yet isolated that particular hip-hop megastar from his former years.

To be fair, perhaps Skinner is only too aware of this ominous overhang. While 50 Cent and Eminem hang out, Skinner is concerned about more mundane realities.

"Whenever Mike Skinner opines on a subject, people listen."

He also told *Rolling Stone* that, 'I was (once) closer to 50 Cent than you are to me now. It was in a London club, and no one in his entourage was pushing me away. What's he spending, thirty grand a day on bodyguards? I could've gotten a knife in that club easily and killed him. I brushed past him on the way to the bathroom. It's good that I'm not a complete psycho who wanted to kill 50 Cent.'

Speaking of Eminem, Skinner is now tired of hearing that he is 'the British Slim Shady' etc etc. At first Skinner acknowledged it was a reasonable comparison to make, saying 'I'd rather be compared to Eminem than to Vanilla Ice'. He also said, 'it would be perverse not to think he's great ... he's always got something to prove and that's what makes someone go from being a good artist to being a great artist. You just can't knock his consistency.'

He's even admitted that Shady has infected his actual writing approach at times, revealing to MTV that, "The Real Slim Shady' was in my head when I wrote ['Too Much Brandy']. Even though it sounds a bit like that record, it's a hell of a lot more that's mine. I'd go toe-to-toe with Eminem anytime.' Yet, as previously touched upon, it was matters far closer to home that were the central core of that tune. That song is just an honest reflection of a night out with Skinner & Co. "Six of us lads came to New York last year and got thrown out of

> *" These are all stories that are taken from my life, rearranged a bit. "*

three places. When we drink beer, some of my mates get hectic. One of them ended up starting a fight with the security staff, and in England they give you a proper beating down if you do that. Here they just tossed us out. It was a flashy place with proper people with proper haircuts. We didn't really belong … These are all stories that are taken from my life, rearranged a bit.'

However, a passing compliment though it may be, there are few real valid comparisons with Mike and Marshall. When Skinner travels to the US, that is the American media's way of quantifying this strange being that has landed on their shores, a little like converting everything back into dollars before they buy it. In the UK, by contrast, the comparison quickly faded as it became apparent that Mike Skinner was very much his own man.

Lyrically speaking at least, Mike is polar opposites to Eminem in many ways. Once again he is brave enough to stand against much of the accepted protocols of a medium he is admittedly obsessed with. 'What you find with a lot of rappers,' he told *The Observer*'s Ben Thompson 'is they work out their flow – the rhythm to their words – and the better they get, the more tidy the flow becomes, until everything has to fit in, the same way it would with a poem. But I tend to think that if it all gets too tidy, the words don't really stick in your mind when you hear them - the smoothness of the rhythm makes you lose concentration.'

Paradoxically, Mike will struggle to deny he is part of a great British heritage of songwriters who have been able to somehow perfectly capture the lifestyle of this spectred isle. Although Morrissey was at times almost imperceptibly similar to Graham Fellows' brilliant comic invention John Shuttleworth (write a set of lyrics down by each and tell them apart), he is also acknowledged by most as a true Brit genius. Suggs is the same, so is Damon from Blur. Ray Davies, Ian Dury. And Mike Skinner. On the surface, the detail they use in their words – food, clothes, slang and so on – is the obvious common denominator but there is something more subtle, an underlying sense of the quintessentially British. The good, the bad and the ugly.

Mind you, there was ample evidence to say that any such similarities with some of his Brit-forefathers was purely coincidental. Back in September 2002, The Streets had performed a one-off show at the London Hammersmith Working Men's Club and Blur vocalist Damon Albarn was at the show. He approached Skinner afterwards but did not perhaps have the effect he might be used to: 'I didn't really know who he was. He was just like, "Welcome to being famous" or something ... I was just like, "Oh, shut up, you pansy." He seems all right, but he's just a different kind of person from me. I kinda get on the train and go see my girlfriend and get on with makin' the music.'

As for garage, which by the time Skinner was enjoying such chart success and critical acclaim had long since past its sell-by date as far as the media was concerned ... Mike knew he possessed that favourite of record company words: longevity. 'When you say "longevity",' he explained to the press, 'you're talking about appealing to people outside of the garage scene. Yeah, I've got more longevity because I've satisfied people from a different background. But the people from London that started garage are still living that life and haven't stopped listening to it. They aren't concerned about people outside of the scene.'

CHAPTER 6: WHERE THE STREET'S HAS NO FAME

'To be honest I think the British are much better at doing drugs and drinking than Americans. Americans are all soft when it comes to taking drugs. The English can really do it.'

Not Tipper Gore. Mike Skinner.

One of the greatest ironies of The Streets' success is that for someone who is lauded for being acutely original and innovative, Mike Skinner rarely features in any article – or indeed this book – without being compared to another artist or writer. Depending on your media preference, the influences/

parallels will differ. The broadsheets have dripped echoes of Alan Bennett, Chaucer, Alan Parker, Dostoevsky, hell even Shakespeare with alarming regularity; the tabloids are more prone to still hail him as the UK's answer to Eminem. At the risk of muddying already teeming waters, I'd like to suggest a new comparative theory to muse over, mainly for people with nothing better to do: the closest kinship The Streets shares with any other current act is the hard dance ubermeisters, The Prodigy.

For one, both acts made their debut albums in their own homes: Prodigy songwriter Liam Howlett as a teenage Essex rave kid gone awry on a £900 Roland W90; Skinner likewise in his bedroom after those years of apeing black American rappers; Secondly, both The Prodigy and Skinner have made people re-evaluate how samples are used in modern music. Howlett's seminal 'Firestarter' was actually partly centred around an Art of Noise sample which had itself been over-used many times before Howlett's own completely fresh incarnation. Skinner's choices are at times more obtuse but no less inspired; thirdly, they are both a very English phenomenon, at least in terms of their sound – while The Prodigy somehow managed to translate this little island parochialism to the USA (and indeed the world) on 1997's ten-million-plus-selling *Fat of the Land*, becoming in the process only the then-seventh UK band to enter the US *Billboard* charts at Number 1, Skinner has a long way to go. The far greater lyrical content and linguistic slant has meant Americans, basically, don't usually understand a word he is saying (although this never seemed to hurt REM). Despite this Anglo-centric sound, they both make no secret of their infatuation with American artists. Paradoxically at least on this count, Howlett has chosen to draw increasing numbers of collaborators onto his work, to the degree that on 2004's long-awaited *Always Outnumbered, Never Outgunned*, so many diverse 'extras' appeared on the album that he did not even utilise his own fiercesome pairing of Keith Flint and Maxim. Skinner is more of a musical loner – even his dabbles with the earnest and mighty Coldplay would never surface (more of which later). Further, although he still admires the work of rappers such as Redman and Nas (and is said to have politely declined collaboration requests from luminaries

"They are both a very English phenomenon, at least in terms of their sound"

such as Outkast), he acknowledges readily that they would be unlikely to fit in with his style of writing and music. He told *CMJ* magazine that, 'The strength of The Streets is the unique focus of the music — a single vision. As fun and creative as collaborations can be, they're never really focused. That's why you get rap songs that have a theme that's about one thing and various verses from various rappers that mean different things. You can't get a group of people together and come up with one thing, because it's quite boring.'

And, one final morsel of comparison, both The Prodigy and The Streets draw more from the punk heritage when they play live than they do from the sub-genre's from whence they crawled. Punk has more to do with a Prodigy and The Streets gig than either rave or garage, by the admission of both acts. It will be interesting to see if The Streets can emulate The Prodigy in this way – the Essex band used their volatile and breath-taking live show to take the world by storm in the late 90s, not least at an array of festivals where captive audiences in the tens of thousands fell at their feet. Can Skinner do the same? Will other major acts ask to be slotted in as second on the bill instead of headline because they don't want to follow The Streets, as has often happened with The Prodigy? Only time will tell.

The point about all these myriad comparisons made with Mike Skinner's work and other artists, writers, playwrights and so on is ... choose your own poison. Do you agree with this new analogy? Does it matter? No, but it's harmless so why not have a go? As Elvis Costello once said, 'Writing about music is like dancing about architecture.'

Will Mike Skinner aka The Streets crack the USA?

Probably not.

I hope I am painfully wrong, because a large dose of Skinnerisms firing up the *Billboard* charts would be one of the most entertaining developments in the music industry for years.

Original Pirate Material was signed to Vice Records in the land of the stars and stripes, and released fully eight months after the album first surfaced in the UK. It was a further six months before the US got to see 'Mikey' in person. He started off over the Atlantic with seven dates in March 2003, starting in Los Angeles' El Rey Theatre and ending at the equally modest Miami Ultra Music Festival. Along the way, he took in an appearance on *The Tonight Show With Jay Leno*, and the not insubstantial accolade of being voted 'Best Debut Album' no less by *Rolling Stone*, as mentioned. Further, the *New York Times* declared that a 'white Briton has made the year's most exciting hip-hop album.' So, in theory, a great start.

However, it probably isn't going to be a walk in the (Central) Park. Despite Mike sharing a DNA-strand with the *Billboard*-topping Prodigy, Howlett's Essex mob had fewer words on their albums than Skinner does in one song. They did, indeed, crack America, at least with one album and countless sell-out tours. It is a sad reality that despite numerous headlines announcing various UK bands have 'cracked' the States, the reality is usually

" Will other major acts ask to be slotted in as second on the bill instead of headline because they don't want to follow The Streets?"

a brief stint in the lower reaches of the *Billboard* listings before a long tour bus journey on to the next club show. Despite its status as an on-going obsession for British acts to 'crack' America, it just doesn't happen very often. 'But what about U2?' They're Irish.

Spice Girls did it, Depeche Mode did it, so did the Floyd, Rod Stewart, Radiohead, Coldplay are in the process of doing so, there was some floppy-haired four piece from Liverpool who once had every Top 5 single in the US charts one week and … so on. It is an elite list. At one point, the US was so concerned about the influx of British beat groups that they restricted the number of work permits to UK bands hoping to tour there – bands that the British Prime Minister Harold MacMillan had called his 'secret weapon'. Unfortunately, during several weeks of 2003 and 2004, there was not one single British act in the *Billboard* Top 100.

Historically, the odds are against Mike Skinner. Specifically, his prospects look even worse. For a start, he has been cursed with the titular postscript that is almost like a death-warrant for British acts – in many parts of the land of the free he is known as The Streets UK. Likewise Suede UK, for example, who evaporated in America like so much cigarette stub smoke.

> *"Yet with The Streets, put forward by many commentators as 'hip-hop' to this market, there's not a 'ho' in sight, bitches would only be American Pit Bulls and caps are something you wear on your head."*

Linguistically, seducing the US with his lyrics is not going to be easy. One magazine suggested his videos were subtitled, another ran a 'Streets Dictionary', which helpfully translated such terms as 'quaffing beer', going to 'the loo', 'chasing brown' and 'rhubarb and custard' etc etc. Another writer said '*Original Pirate Material* can be as difficult to get through as *A Clockwork Orange*.' Not that hip-hop itself doesn't come with its own vernacular, but the crucial difference is that US audiences are used to that, they know the phrases, the street slang, it is all familiar. Yet with The Streets, put forward by many commentators as 'hip-hop' to this market, there's not a 'ho' in sight, bitches would only be American Pit Bulls and caps are something you wear on your head.

Mike's own theory – and it is probably a valid one – is that UK audiences watch so much American TV that any popular colloquialisms or slang terms quickly get consumed into the current UK lexicon; by contrast, US audiences rarely watch UK shows … *Eastenders* being the obvious example of failure, *The Office* being a rare exception. Consequently, when a musician turns up talking in UK slang or about uniquely British experiences, essentially the US listener hasn't got a clue what he is talking about. And when that artist is delivering a narrative-led set of songs, understanding what he is saying is fairly central to the whole point. Add to that Skinner's odd London–Brummie hybrid accent and in certain US states you might as well release a song in Chinese.

Plus, America is the hip-hop and rap homeland, where those genres are the biggest selling musical off-shoots in the States, bar only country music. Which in itself should tell you something. While Radiohead's uniquely bloated-yet-brilliant modern prog was irresistible to a market where there was nothing like that out there, or where The Prodigy's hard dance captured the very zeitgeist of a post-Nirvana youth, Mike Skinner is competing against, literally, hundreds of thousands of acts in his genre.

By contrast, maybe he is not competing in that genre at all. Notably, The Streets' being pigeon-holed as 'alternative' by many US radio programmers and industry observers had a visible impact on the demograph of his live audience in America. While there was always going to be far more hip-hop in Skinner's music than anything to do with Radiohead or the typically 'indie' US college circuit, Mike's cohort Kevin Mark Trail was frequently the only black person in the entire venue.

Add to that the fact that America's number one spectator sport in terms of live attendance – Nascar racing – has one leading light called ... Mike Skinner. You can buy Mike Skinner T-shirts, novelty cups and helmets. Telling his millions of fans that there is another Mike Skinner they should be listening to instead would be like trying to launch a yodelling pop star called The David Beckham. It gets worse. There is even a musician called Michael Skinner. After a successful career playing drums and guitars for various rock acts including American Train, Michael Skinner went solo and, to confuse matters still further, released among several albums, one called *Pirates*.

Then there's Mike's teeth. They are crooked, not pearly white. He can't be serious about his music if his teeth aren't all ship-shape and Bristol fashion. Not in America. After all, Ronan Keating had his teeth done, he's got a fine grill now ... oh, no he didn't break America either. Still, Mike's got the money now, so he really should pop down the dentist. It's the least he could do.

All in all, The Streets' Mike Skinner is not blessed with an easy ride in the USA. His chances don't look good.

Not that he actually seems to care.

'In America they have this [negative] association in their mind,' he told Gil Kaufman of MTV, 'with dance music or the rave culture. But it's been our street culture for fifteen years. I've made a record in England for English people. One day they phoned me up and said, "Do you fancy going to New York and talking about yourself and getting free trainers?" So, I can't understand why anyone in America would want to get into it. Americans are insular — they don't need to go outside America for anything. They're not ready for it.' He openly states he hates what George Bush stands for, but admires the American thirst for success and the mentality that supports winners, not underdogs/failures.

> *"Then there's Mike's teeth. They are crooked, not pearly white. He can't be serious about his music if his teeth aren't all ship-shape and Bristol fashion."*

Skinner, admirably, declined the fawning interest of numerous major record labels in the US to instead sign to that smaller independent, Vice. Surely correctly, he was convinced that if he signed for mega-bucks with a biggie, the idiosyncrasies of his records would quickly be stifled by the pressure of the dollar and he would end up a negative figure on a profit-and-loss sheet. So that's why, perceptively, he chose to go with the highly reputable Vice. He knew they would back him up, inject his US campaign with passion and arguably give him his best chance over in the US. He is realistic about what to expect too – he acknowledges that the UK will always be his key territory and says he doesn't mind at all if the US don't take to him.

But what about touring your arse off like Bono and pals until the nation is bludgeoned into submission and the heartlands sell-out cowsheds in minutes? Not for this particular UK garage head. Who does he tour the US with? A radio-friendly Americanised MOR act to soften the underbelly of the cynical Yanks? Nope. He takes Dizzee Rascal with him on the plane, arguably one of the few artists in the UK at that time whose incredible talent is so immersed in British street culture that he is even more unpalatable to the myopic American music industry. Before 'Dry Your Eyes' had

"I was a bit too drunk. I was a bit out of order. If I'm honest, I was a cunt onstage."

elevated Mike to superstar status back home, the unlikely pairing headed out to the US for a series of fourteen dates, with five sharing the bill together at such salubrious venues as Montreal Club Soda. To be fair, they would also play New York's Irving Plaza but other than that, it was hardly an arena tour. Maybe that would come ...

Showing blunt honesty that some US audiences don't quite understand, Skinner was very frank when asked to summarise one set of gigs in America: San Francisco was 'a bit lukewarm, Chicago was rowdy ... but (in New York) I was a bit too drunk. I was a bit out of order. If I'm honest, I was a cunt onstage.'

Despite all this, *Original Pirate Material* somehow managed to hit the US Top 30, so maybe Mike has something to look forward to after all. Let's hope so.

Watching life go by, summer 2002.

The Holloway Road, home to Nick Worthington's record shop and Mike Skinner's launchpad into the spotlight.

Chilling just after the release of *Original Pirate Material*, spring 2002.

Getting The Drinks In, live on stage.

As close as you can get to Mike Skinner's Vauxhall home,
near to the MI6 building in south London.

Dizzee Rascal in 2005.

Skinner's antecedents on Radio Caroline,
illegally transmitting back in 1964.

Skinner's nearest relatives?
The original Prodigy line-up pictured in 1998.

Skinner's biggest hip-hop influence, the Wu Tang Clan.

At the Reading Festival, August, 2003.

Performing at Irving Plaza, New York, 30th June, 2004.

Turning his back on convention during his
Brit Awards performance, February 2005.

A Vauxhall Chavalier at a Chav Rally, organised by Goldie Lookin' Chain
to promote their single, 'Your Mother's Got A Penis.'

Mike Skinner trying to get his head around his success.

At the risk of repeating myself, to see The Streets atop the US charts, with magazines filled with adverts for jeans and 'men's fragrances' containing articles explaining the finer points of his own London-Birmingham-Esperanto, would just about be one of music's most bizarre and yet utterly welcome sights. Fingers crossed.

CHAPTER 7:
SHIT, BUT
YOU SHOW IT

'If I was a girl, I'd rather fuck a rock star than a plumber.'

Not Mike Skinner, not Tipper Gore, but Kiss frontman Gene Simmons who, coincidentally, can never get a decent plumber round.

After two years in the making, Mike Skinner put the finishing touches to his second album, to be called *A Grand Don't Come For Free* in March 2004. The by-now highly anticipated album was scheduled for release in the second week of May that year. Three weeks earlier, Mike unleashed his opening volley, the first single. A classic by the name of 'Fit, But You Know It'.

His record company must have been jumping through hoops with joy when they heard the proposed first single. Barely a sniff of garage in sight. This was the Sex Pistols doing garage. Rampant guitar riffing throughout, again a typical Skinner single guitar phrase, repeated over and over to massive effect. The elements we expected from the debut album were all there – the fast food scenario, the spoken-word mixed ultra-high in the mix, the soulful chorus courtesy of Calvin, the devastating eye for detail and the numerous characters pitching into the scene.

Yet somehow, it felt like a progression. Better, more sophisticated. Of course, it helped the forthcoming album's campaign no end that the song was perfect for radio, that the summer was coming and the foreign holiday that Skinner was talking about was already being booked by millions in sweaty anticipation. What a way to come back, a killer track and strategically, in terms of market positioning and selling records, absolutely spot-on.

The lines between fiction and autobiography are always going to be blurred with an artist like Skinner; likewise, Eminem aka Slim Shady aka Marshall Mathers seems to have more split personalities than Hannibal Lecter. However, Mike was eager to distance himself from the infidelity and intrigue that peppers the single 'Fit …' While the UK tabloid press effectively announced that the song was entirely autobiographical, even citing numerous examples from his own real-life relationships, Skinner begged to differ: 'My songs have no relevance to my real life. If I was to have a really big argument with my girlfriend, I wouldn't be so stupid to put it in a song would I?'

Mike Skinner is more than just a rapper. His entire package – with the possible exception, for now, of his live act – is one coherent canvas, with each section he creates adding to the whole. The music is the centre of his palette, obviously, but he seems able to add to the portrait with various other media – his official website is one of the few artist sites that you can actually go to and browse, or better still be taken through a wet, windy, downbeat, visual journey through his music. Best of all though are his videos and it is here, both with 'Fit …' and his other promotional clips that Skinner is continuing a tradition of great British acts such as Blur who have been able to extend their output beyond solely audio.

"Mike Skinner is more than just a rapper. His entire package – with the possible exception, for now, of his live act – is one coherent canvas."

The video for 'Fit …' is a simple idea, but one that is delivered with some panache. Skinner has returned from the sun-kissed result of a fortnight's holiday and goes to collect his holiday snaps. While walking back home, he is unable to wait and begins flicking through the visual vignettes, that then proceed to spring to real life before your very eyes, thus telling the tale of the single. We have the chip shop, the birds and the blokes, the beer, it's all there. Even a passport photo booth shot of a girl, complete with guilty/'whatever!' smirk from Skinner.

The filming for the Club 18-30-style video saw the star nearly cripple himself. They were shooting a scene by a swimming pool and Mike was mucking about and having a laugh when he ran to dive in the pool, slipped and cracked his back on the tiles, knocking all the wind out of himself and perhaps giving an even bigger fright to his record company and video director. Fortunately, he dragged himself up and recovered, and who knows, perhaps that incident added an essential element of physicality to his tired and partied-out appearance in the video clip.

The music stations loved the video, radio loved the track and barely an hour went by in that month of release when you didn't hear it blasting out of someone's radio or TV. The result? A new entry at Number 5 in April 2004. Skinner was back and in business.

A fortnight abroad is a staple part of the British youth. Maybe it is the pent-up expression of just 3.8% of the working year taken as holiday, 336 hours from start to finish in which to enjoy every Bacchanalian excess on offer. Maybe they just want a good time. It is an unadulterated rites of passage for millions every year and a fact of British life. As such, this wasn't the first time that such 'forin 'olidays' had been the subject of a song. The last band who had so perfectly captured the crude *joi de vie* of two-weeks' beer-swilling, bird-shagging, drug-taking, bloke-pulling, vomit-spewing, hotel-trashing holiday in the Med, was Blur with their hit single 'Girls And Boys. The 18-30 carnage that will forever besmirch the Brit-abroad was encapsulated beautifully by mid-Britpop Albarn and Co.

Back in March 1994, Blur had sent us scurrying back for our early 80s electro disco pop collection, rooting out our dust-covered Giorgio Moroder and Sparks records. 'Girls And Boys' opened with a rinky dink riff and then a robotic drum machine beat which crashed in with one of Britpop's finest bass leads, quirky phased guitars and oddly infectious yet humourously mechanical keyboards.

Lyrically the song was an ambiguous celebration of the fuck 'n' chuck mentality of those notorious 18–30 style vacations. Lines about "battery thinkers, count their thoughts on 1, 2, 3, 4 , 5 fingers" and "du bist sehr schon, but we haven't been introduced" captured the meat market scenarios perfectly. Then there was the chorus – "girls who are boys who like boys to be girls who do boys like they're girls who do girls like they're boys". To complete the package, the sleeve artwork was taken from a cheap packet of condoms. Blur had released a gem of a single that suddenly catapulted them past all their contemporaries. This was unquestionably Blur's finest and most audacious moment so far.

The single secured massive radio play nationwide as all manner of broadcasting policies found something in the single that fitted with their play lists. 'Single of the Week' awards flooded in and Blur were suddenly splashed across a multitude of magazine covers, who were coincidentally covering Kurt Cobain's suicide. The parallels with Skinner are obvious; what both songs did was take each band on to a new level.

There were few doubters and critics of The Streets' opening single from the second album, but there were some whispers among observers that the song's singalong 'yob-appeal' might be misconstrued and lead The Streets into a corner of yobbish caricature ... but then, people didn't know what Mike had up his sleeve next ...

Aside from chattering about his first Top 5 hit, both media observers and the public alike were also intrigued by the rumours that Mike Skinner and Coldplay's Chris Martin were collaborating on a forthcoming song. For someone who was known to generally shun collaborations, especially high profile ones, Skinner's choice of Chris Martin to work with on soon-to-be-massive-anyway track 'Dry Your Eyes' was certainly an eyebrow-raiser. After all, one half of this oddball duo openly spoke about getting mashed, while the other, more 'Hollywood' half was famed for not drinking, smoking, drugging, or generally partying at all. Even Martin's first born child was named after a fruit.

Bearing in mind that the public had not at this stage heard the actual track, the original recorded version of 'Dry Your Eyes' had Martin's famously melancholic vocals on the chorus, but Skinner ultimately released the track with his a new set of vocals replacing Mr Paltrow's. However, inevitably, media and public interest in this most unlikely of partnerships was sufficient that the saga did not end there.

Rumours circulated that the Martin vocal version was available on the internet, the first resort for the 21st century bootlegger. The theory was that an American radio had somehow got hold of a copy and that a download was available. It was also unclear as to why the collaboration did not ultimately come out, although Skinner was happy to offer his own thoughts: "There's another company that owns the copyright on his voice and that's a very big company,' he explained to writer Vicky Roberts. 'I sent it in, I went over to Camden and recorded it in their studio with my laptop and then I took it back and mixed it and finished it and sent it back to his label and all we really heard was, 'No it's not really working', so I don't really know really. I get the impression that he didn't like the sound of his voice on it or that his record label didn't want it to happen." Elsewhere, on NME.com, Skinner had this to say about what was arguably to become the album's biggest track: "Dry Your Eyes' is the moment of complete panic when your girlfriend finishes with you ... it's a sad one.' As for the track being 'his ballad', Skinner was a little startled, as he told *Notion* magazine: 'To me it didn't sound like a

> *"Skinner's choice of Chris Martin to work with on soon-to-be-massive-anyway track 'Dry Your Eyes' was certainly an eyebrow-raiser."*

ballad. I just never thought of that word! It was just a slow pop song that was quite sad. When people started calling it a ballad, I was thinking, "Oh, my God, what have I done?!"'

For his own part, Martin was suitably understated, telling Harborough FM's Thom Costall: 'Well it's an interesting story if you're into Coldplay and if you're not it's really boring, but ... there was this version of it which I sang the chorus. But I said I didn't think it was as good as the version where he sang the chorus. Then he didn't think that was as good as the version where some other dude sang the chorus, so neither him nor me sing on the chorus.' He went on to say, 'But it was cool to spend the day with him. He's an amazing guy; you know there are some great rappers coming out. I don't know whether he'd class himself as a rapper or a MC or whatever.'

New father Chris Martin also highlighted the size of the actual gulf between him and Mike Skinner by closing with, 'If someone told me my life at the moment would be changing nappies and writing lyrics I would've taken it, y'know? It's my dream come true.'

Ironically, Martin had bemused observers when, days after his baby Apple arrived, his band's official website ran a video of a 'spoof' band called The Nappies, allegedly signed to Coldplay's label, complete with heavy-metal wigs and a crap song. Apparently oblivious

> *"I had to pull my sister away and we went home. Plus I never spoke with Chris ever again. I don't quite know where to hide my face, ya know."*

to any relevance to the recent match-up with Skinner, Martin said, 'I think every white guy growing up in Devon dreams of being able to rap, and that's why we signed The Nappies – it was something that we could never be. But it's just that single track, now everyone's got to forget about them.'

With poetic accuracy, Mike and Chris Martin had a not-so-perfect night out not long after their attempted collaboration. Mike took his sister along and, according to him, she got really drunk. Eventually, a glass of wine was spilt. 'I had to pull my sister away and we went home. Plus I never spoke with Chris ever again. I don't quite know where to hide my face, ya know.'

Whatever the reason for the much-hyped collaboration's no-show, it is a shame that this record never saw the light of day as a general release; having said that, with the juggernaut success of Skinner's final version about to swamp The Streets and change Mike's career – and life – forever, it may just have been a lucky twist of fate.

Maybe with Chris Martin the track might not have managed to wriggle its way through the corporate game of snakes and ladders that weigh down celebrity collaborations; maybe the public would have not taken to the partnership; maybe the use of a celebrity vocal within the context of the second album's most poignant and ultra-real track could have been a perceived misjudgement that left the public unmoved and their wallets firmly in their pockets. Who knows? It is all conjecture.

What is a fact is that The Streets chose to release their own version and things would never be the same again.

CHAPTER 8:
SGT PEPPER'S VILLAGE GREEN TALES FROM THE TOPOGRAPHIC ZEN ARCADE IN THE WEE SMALL HOURS CLUB BAND

maverick :~ a local term to describe an unbranded calf or yearling which has no mark of ownership; by the 1860s the phrase had come to represent a person who is considered a dissenter, an independent with no particular attachment to a place or group.

Dictionary of Word Origins by
Linda and Roger Flavell.

As with his first album, Skinner decided to only release one single before putting out the album. A confident man. As the waiting press pack and an expectant public eagerly rubbed their hands at the thought of Skinner's forthcoming new album, on the music grapevine there came news of a dreadful development. His second album was, gulp, a concept album.

Concept albums. Long hair. Gatefold sleeves, loon pants, sequined blusher, 128- track mixing desks, album budgets that read like phone numbers, prog rock, the mighty Rick Wakeman, Yes, Pink Floyd ad nauseum. You know the score, you just don't like to listen to it. And now Mike Skinner, The Streets was about to release a concept album, allegedly. It all made for very uncomfortable reading for followers of the UK's most street-cool new act in years.

Let's look at the facts. Most concept albums are shit. Some aren't, I'll give you that. Many music writers cite The Beatles' *Sgt Pepper's Lonely Hearts Club Band* as the first concept album, partly due to the two versions of the title track which wrap around the album – although actually many of the songs are unrelated. Perhaps more true to the notion of an album's 'concept' came in the same year as *Sgt Pepper*, 1967, with the record *S.F. Sorrow* by the Pretty Things, which told the entire story of the eponymous character. The Who also released a vaguely concept album that year called *The Who Sell Out*, which oddly enough was about a pirate radio station that only played Who music (they furthered the cause with *Tommy* and arguably *Quadrophenia*) Taking it back further, some observers credit ol' blue eyes himself, Frank Sinatra, with the first concept album, when he released 1955's *In The Wee Small Hours*, on which all the tracks centred around the theme of separated lovers; a more popular theory jumps forward nearly two decades to Yes's 1973 opus, *Tales From Topographic Oceans*, as probably the first concept album, centred as it was around based on the four part Hindu Shastric scriptures.

If you find yourself with nothing to do except dull your senses, then a trawl through the history of concept albums might take you to any of the following: pretty much anything by Frank Zappa, Marillion, Yes, Jethro Tull, Fairport Convention, Jefferson Airplane, *The Village Green Preservation Society* by The Kinks, Marvin Gaye's Motown-genre-busting *What's Going On* and so on ... Oh, don't forget Emerson, Lake & Palmer. And Hawkwind. If you can bear it.

"When word spread that The Streets' much-anticipated second album sounded like a concept record, the signs weren't good."

One of the few recent precedents with a shred of credibility was *Zen Arcade* by seminal US band Hüsker Dü from 1984, but that was almost two decades previous; *The Queen is Dead* by The Smiths two years later smacked of concept also. Yes, there is Radiohead's *Kid A* too, from 2003, but I've never actually been able to get right to the end of that so I can't comment.

And as for 2000's *Machina* by The Smashing Pumpkins, well, I wouldn't even try to. The very nearest contemporary to Skinner's second album was the laugh-a-minute epic in 2003 called *De-Loused in the Comatorium* by The Mars Volta, wherein a man fails in his attempted morphine overdose, slips into a deep coma plagued by hellish visions then reawakens and decides he wanted to die after all.

So, when word spread that The Streets' much-anticipated second album sounded like a concept record, the signs weren't good. As the above catalogue of horrors testifies, there was just so little to find positives in. Look up the words 'concept album' anywhere – web, encyclopaedia, magazine, take your pick – and you are unlikely to find the words 'credible', 'modern' or 'remotely worthy of using up vinyl or CD-plastic' anywhere. Well, there's always a first …

Even before the second album was released, Mike was finding himself having to explain the prospect of a concept record. The album's coherent whole belied a more fractured genesis, which Skinner was all too happy to detail to the waiting press hordes. Continuity was there in the shape of most of the album being recorded at home, in this case not his mother's but at his new house, a converted south London (Vauxhall) pub (where else?!). Remarkably, despite his success, his home 'studio' is still as make-shift as ever. There are no sound-proofed £6,000 doors, no state-of-the-art insulation and glass booths; instead in a separate room from his bed (he has graduated from recording in his actual bedroom) the walls are covered in studio foam. Clothes litter the floor and tapes and CDs pile up in uneasy columns. Fortunately, the 'studio' is in the cellar, so there are no neighbours to upset and this proved useful when Mike needed to crank things up a little!

Speaking on London alternative radio Xfm, he said, 'I kinda think (the concept) happened while I was recording it. I've always wanted each song to say something specific but I also like it when songs refer to other tracks. Tracks talking to each other y'know? Then it ended up as this bloody concept album. I hate the word 'concept' though. Makes me think of Spinal Tap.'

He was also aware that the lion's den of critical and public expectation was utterly unforgiving, even so early on in a career. 'I think with the first [album], what I had on my side was that it was such a new idea. That was the impact of that one,' he told *Notion* magazine. 'And I knew that if I'd done that again, people would be like, "Well, we've kind of heard that." The first album was all about going out. This one is kind of the opposite, though, cos I'm not really doing anything the whole album, I'm just sitting in a chair, watching telly!'

Ah, his telly …

He'd lost a thousand pounds you see.

It was on the telly when he last saw it.

Then his mates came round, had a laugh, and then the money wasn't there anymore. A grand don't come for free, these days.

My missus goes down the gym, pounds the treadmill and watches MTV without the sound on. In between being a young mom, looking after her two boys and putting everyone else first. By contrast, I sit in a warm, cocooned room, writing about and listening to music I love. Which gives me no right to preach about what music she should be listening to.

'Look, you should listen to this album, it's unbelievable.'

'When have I got time to sit down and listen to a whole album from start to finish …? Stop bangin' on about it. Besides, if I put The Streets on in the car, God-only knows what the boy will start saying at crèche …'

'How about when you go down the gym? You go on that treadmill for about fifty minutes don't ya?'

'Forty, who do you think I am? Paula Radcliffe?'

'Okay, well maybe push the boat out a bit and run another ten minutes. I guarantee you won't regret it.'

'It can't be that good ... but I'll give it a go, if only to shut you up!'

One hour later.

'Well, what do you think?'

'I think that might just be the best album I've ever heard.'

And so we come to the impossible. Writing about something that is best enjoyed by being listened to. Reviewing an album that is one of the defining moments in British music history. Mike Skinner's second album as The Streets: *A Grand Don't Come For Free*.

From the very first line, you knew it was going to work. Trumpeting fanfares and Mike's doleful voice piles into a word-heavy lyric within seconds of 'It Was Supposed To Be So Easy'. Skinner is taking his DVD back, getting some cash and sorting out his savings, before having tea with his mom. Simple stuff. Not for Mike. The mundanity of the album's opening track is stark, but in a sense that tells you that this is going to be no ordinary hip-hop-inspired album. He still has the lolloping beats in there, some odd electronic background sounds and his trademark strings.

The chorus is typical Skinner – oddly syncopated delivery, chopping up everyday words and stressing different parts of the word to the norm, squashing them into a rhyme but never sounding forced. And his acute observations are still there – who hasn't sworn at their mobile phone in *exactly* the same way Mike does in this song? With 'It Was Supposed To Be So Easy', the scene is set. His thousand pounds going missing is just the final insult in a day when everything goes wrong.

Then Mike brings it straight down on track two, future single 'Could Well Be In'. The simple electronic drumbeat and plodding, descending piano phrase keeps the song musically very basic. However, the lyrics are

"The chorus is typical Skinner – oddly syncopated delivery, chopping up everyday words and stressing different parts of the word to the norm, squashing them into a rhyme but never sounding forced."

again the focus, almost melody free and effectively spoken-word. Then the chorus arrives with its injection of slang comedy. You can see Skinner sitting in front of *Trisha* or Lorraine Kelly listening intently to the 'dating' advice. We've all seen the shows, we just haven't made Top 40 singles out of them (the album's fourth and final single in November 2004, reaching Number 30).

Of course, the track deftly introduces Simone into the theatre. She may look well rough, but Mike's affection for her is very clear. She may chat on her mobile for ages while he picks at beer labels and tries not to look disowned, but he is keen, nonetheless. A sister song for 'Don't Mug Yourself' maybe, but already, two songs in, the narrative is developing effortlessly.

'***Not Addicted***' brazenly confronts Mike's

interest in gambling in a harshly-delivered, oddly sound-tracked account of an afternoon in a bookies. Perhaps one of the album's least appealing, ominous-sounding tunes, the lyrics are darkly comical, seeing Mike betting on football, which he admits he knows nothing about. When this goes awry, he switches to cricket, about which he knows even less. This tune might not add to the romantic element of the album, but what it does is colour his world, complete with the background voices advising him not to put money down, chattering in the corners of the smoke-filled bookies where he spends a lot of his week. This is a tune that draws most obvious comparisons with Ken Loach. There's something perfect about Skinner's choice of vice – not hard drugs, alcohol, all the staples of rock and roll, but gambling on footy, cricket, anything. He's not addicted though.

Then it's 'Blinded By The Lights', the album's first classic tune. Another simple beat, single snare, sparse bass drum, gently rising strings before the song's signature stabbing keyboard stabs. It all sounds so *dark*. Skinner seems to possess the ability to capture on record the exact experience of going to a shoddy, sweaty club. The detail is there again, taking you through sending a text, going to the door to get a signal, not getting served quickly, once again we have all been there.

The female lead vocal lifts the darkness but sounds eerie, unsettling, evoking snippets of garage or house songs that so often ram home the chorus with just such a rabble-rousing female lead. But by then, the second pill is taking effect, Mike is mashed and the whole song is like being strapped inside Skinner's skull, a fly-on-the-brain's-wall. Simone wasn't where she said she would be, there is a hint of intrigue as she seems to be unnecessarily close to Dan, Skinner is fighting off the effects of brandy and ecstasy (brilliantly captured by keyboard whooshes and a skipping hi-hat, reminiscent of Mike's palpitating heart) trying to cranc his neck to see what is going on. A genius track, which hit Number 10 on its September 2004 release as a single.

Then Mike skits across back to his house, roaching a spliff, watching the telly. The tedium is almost tangible. 'Wouldn't Have It Any Other Way' is most notable for Calvin Schmalvin's soulful vocals, which sit over Skinner's monotone narrative which, for once, is somewhat droning. By now, it appears that Mike is becoming infatuated with Simone, an emotion fuelled by being stoned, telling the world how much he loves her while *Eastenders* or *The Bill* are on in the background. Calvin's closing R&B vocal is hilarious, detailing not heartache, not some dull emotion, but cleaning the ashtray and clipper.

Then, bang, we are into this album's 'The Irony Of It All', a comic masterpiece, brilliantly composed and delivered by the name of 'Get Out Of My House'. This is just a straight comedy sketch, finding Mike cornered by Simone without much of an answer. Her accent is so thick, dense, but when added to the stomping beats and heavy bass seems to be the only vocal that would do. All the time, a powerless Mike vainly tries to defend himself in the background. The closing one-way spoken word argument is pure drama, and could just as easily have been an award-winning TV show.

The middle-eight is a classic, perhaps the best comic moment on the record. This is also the song where it is revealed that Mike is actually epileptic. The duality of those two contrasting elements is a brave step, but

Skinner fears nothing when he is on this sort of form. It is also the song when you start to think that maybe Simone is, as my mother said, 'no good for him anyway.'

Then the centre of the album fires us right up with the aforementioned 'Fit, But You Know It', the most 'pop' song on the record. Taken within the context of the album's narrative, it is even better.

The crudely-titled 'Such A Twat' sees Skinner coming home from his debauched holiday, although his hangover is dealt with by swigging Chardonnays from mini-size bottles offered by the wary stewardesses. Mike is guilty about his sunshine infidelity, and paranoid that Simone will finish with him as a result. Here he is, confessing on his mobile phone – complete with signal break-ups – to a mate. It was the aftershots, the ice cream, the fact he thought they might be finished, honest. Then the revelation that the nine-and-a-half-after-four-beers woman actually wasn't even that good-looking. All recounted in a corner of his kitchen where he gets his best signal on his phone. How he thinks this stuff up is beyond me.

The intrigue and scheming is ramped up immediately on 'What Is He Thinking?', when Skinner is wondering why his friend Scott seems so fidgety and uneasy around him. His coat has mysteriously returned, he must have stolen it, so why not assume it was Scott that took the thousand pounds too?

The music is B-movie horror soundtrack, but it never sounds cheap. There are brass stabs, dark strings and thumping bass, all blended seamlessly. Scott's vocals are perfect, just about shaking with an edge of nervousness. This is when we start to realise that Simone is playing away and that Scott knows who with.

Yet Skinner is still barking up the wrong path, while Scott is frightened that he will find out. Then the revelation that rocks Mike's world ... the thousand pounds, the coat, the holiday, everything doesn't matter ... Simone is seeing Dan.

Then the sweeping strings introduce us to both the album's strongest song, arguably Skinner's finest moment to date and without doubt the track that would alter his world forever: 'Dry Your Eyes'. Simone knows that he knows. She is not interested. Yet, faced with such cold rejection, he still aches for her soft touch, he can't admit it is over. Scott tries to console and advise him, throwing in the blokey 'plenty more fish in the sea' platitude to make him feel better. It doesn't.

"The duality of those two contrasting elements is a brave step, but Skinner fears nothing when he is on this sort of form."

The gently strummed acoustic guitar and sweeping strings ought to be totally at odds with Skinner's rapidly-spoken narrative, but by putting himself high in the mix, yet having recorded his vocal very quietly – particularly when he breaks it down mid-song – the intimacy of the song is crushing. Then, only a few lines later he is swearing again, but this time not out of violence or anger, but out of confusion, out of frustration, out of rejection. This is one of those songs that has entered the psyche of the public and will be played on radio and TV ad infinitum. Even the harshest, most churlish Skinner critic would be hard pushed to deny him this moment of genius.

So then comes the final track, the bizarre closer, 'Empty Cans'. A parallel world with two endings, this song is a masterstroke that brings the concept to a close and drops in the final, devastatingly cunning twist. Skinner is first seen drinking heavily, miserable, self-pitying, shambolic. The TV man is coming round to repair his broken set, but the beer leads to an argument and then a fight. The coarse chorus and harsh words seem disappointing from him, but he is gutted about Simone, he sees no reason to be reasonable.

"On first hearing, you shiver, it is that good"

Then the rewind button is pressed and we start all over again. Suddenly, there is optimism, the hairs on the back of your neck start to rise up, you begin to realise something is coming but you know not what. Skinner slightly alters the music to bring in gentle piano, which instantly changes the atmosphere. He admits his regret, speaks more positively of Scott, understands why his friend didn't tell him sooner ... then the rising strings start the album's climax. Scott comes round and takes the back off the telly to try to fix it (if you haven't heard this song yet then (a) what planet do you come from? and (b) skip to the next paragraph or else I will spoil the ending). There, down the back of the set, is Mike's thousand pounds.

On first hearing, you shiver, it is that good. You want to tell everyone but then tell no one, because you don't

104

want to spoil it for them. How often can you say that about an album?

We leave Skinner chatting with a new girl, Alison, whom he seems to get on with. He is mellower, he knows what has happened and why and the feel-good factor is fantastic. Yet, even here, Skinner tells us he's washed his jeans on too high a temperature and they are a bit tight. Classic.

Then it is over. If that is what a concept album is all about, I'm off to buy Hawkwind's entire back-catalogue.

Once again five★ and 9-out-of-ten reviews were the norm. When set against the enormous press file for *Original Pirate Material*, this was all the more an achievement; it is a rare event when a follow-up to a critically lauded record so easily outperforms its vaunted predecessor.

By the time the critics got hold of *A Grand ...*, being compared to Eminem was the least of Mike Skinner's worries. Easy to scoff at but valid nonetheless, the broadsheets in particular found countless literary comparisons there to be made about Skinner and his work. The phrase 'kitchen sink drama', so associated with writer's such as Alan Bennett, Alan Parker, Sean O' Casey and so on was frequently used. Alan Bennett was an obvious and, to be fair, perfectly reasonable comparison that was made. Shakespeare for the text generation was another. In *The Guardian*, a renowned University College London literature professor wrote 1,800 words dissecting Skinner's lyrics and showing their genealogy to past life literary greats, the main thrust being that Mr Mike was the new Dostoevsky. He also mentioned Samuel Pepys.

One of the broadsheets likened his compositional approach to Francis Bacon. Another writer had this to say: 'To the constant Eminem comparisons, I would say bollocks. Mike Skinner is the new Chaucer. English Literature fans may balk at this suggestion, but his tales are told in a colloquial way and do not spare the facts however grim they might be ... This type of lyrical honesty has seen the Britain of Mike Skinner, the Britain in which a lot of us inhabit, be uncovered in a truly remarkable fashion. This is similar to the way Chaucer exposed the Britain of the medieval times, in the *Canterbury Tales*.

Another literary professor claimed Skinner had produced an album that reflected Christ and 'the lost silver', but Mike was suitably dry when this was pointed out: 'If he reckons that, then yeah. But that's not really what I had in mind.'

There are some dissenting voices: *Guardian* music critic, Caroline Sullivan, dismissed it as 'gormless rap-mumbling' that merely heralded a lifestyle defined by 'aimless rounds of late-night kebabs, spliffs and untaxed Ford Cortinas.' She is in a very small minority, although you have to admire her nerve for writing what she thinks against a barrage of positive acclaim.

Regardless of whether you agree with the majority viewpoint or not, it was all incredible stuff really and Mike, for his part, was not always entirely comfortable with these well-intended and extremely flattering appraisals. 'That's what those kind of people do,' he mused to one magazine, 'they analyze everything. It's not a bad thing, it's just what they do. Whereas, often, most people aren't analyzing it like that.'

Most people were too busy buying it, listening to it

and telling their mates to buy it. *A Grand Don't Come For Free* sold very strongly from day one, although like its predecessor this was also to be a slow-burning commercial success.

There were numerous key events which boosted sales of the album. A second nomination for the Mercury Music Prize helped. Despite being the pre-match bookies favourite at 3-1, Skinner was, perhaps not surprisingly, unimpressed by the hullabaloo and pomp of the forthcoming back-slapping night out. 'People say I snub awards but I don't, I don't go cos

"That's what those kind of people do, they analyze everything. It's not a bad thing, it's just what they do. Whereas, often, most people aren't analyzing it like that."

I don't fit in. The Mercury's are really full on and I didn't realise you're supposed to wear a suit and I turned up in my trainers and cap (last time). I won't go this time, I've been thinking about it, so don't bet on me winning 'cos you don't get an award if you don't go!' Ever the diplomat, he added, 'It is a great award and I'm very proud to be nominated again.'

Brit nominations would follow (more later) and more end-of-year 'Best Album ...' accolades than you can shake a stick at. Already, with only one single taken from the record, *A Grand* ...was being hailed as a success.

Then the second single, 'Dry Your Eyes' was released.

CHAPTER 9:
BLINDED BY THE (LACK OF) SLIGHTS

'I've got a review that calls me a genius right next to one that calls me a jerk.'

Barry Manilow in 1988. Mike Skinner hasn't. Yet.

Looking back, it seems odd that 'Dry Your Eyes', the album's most obvious mainstream song was held back as a second single. After all, the party-hard vibe of Number 5 hit 'Fit, But You Know It' was a brilliant campaign opener, but hardly likely to win over the ever-swelling ranks of Radio 2 listeners and the country's more conservative media spotters that so often hold the key to massive selling albums. The album had sold very strongly in its first few weeks of release, but there was a distinct mellowing of cash-going-through-tills for Mr Skinner.

The concern from his team was that such a powerful

ballad might be mis-interpreted as a 'sell-out' if you will, a play to the middle England listener and if so, would risk a wholesale migration away from the more underground and hardcore fans who had been following Skinner from day one. Then, when the actual content of *A Grand...* became more widely known, these latterday supporters might disown Skinner and he'd be left with neither set of fans. The risk was all the more acute given that releasing 'Dry Your Eyes' as a single was lifting it out of its context within the story of the album. So, 'Fit, But You Know It' was the better choice as opening single, to cement Skinner's foundation fanbase before moving on to more riskier climes. Otherwise, the leap of faith may well have been just too much to ask.

It was not a new tactic – Coldplay released 'In My Place' as the first single from the more experimental and demanding second album *A Rush Of Blood To The Head*, a song which could have easily been a left-over from their debut long player, *Parachutes*. Once that was over, the more obtuse songs such as 'The Scientist' found a much warmer reception in a pre-disposed British public.

You can talk about the strategy of releasing 'Dry Your Eyes' all day, the simple fact is it worked. The public loved the song. Seemingly every radio station played it. Record shops couldn't stack the shelves quick enough. Over 54,000 people bought the single in its first week of release in July 2004, *four times* as many as had bought 'Fit But You Know It'. It entered the charts straight at Number 1.

Of course, with 'Dry Your Eyes' sitting at the top of the charts, there were now hundreds of thousands of people who had previously never heard of Mike – heavy rotation on Steve Wright's Sunday Love Songs on Radio

Two anyone? Now they wanted to know if he had an album out.

He did.

They all bought it.

A Grand ... went to Number 1 in the charts the very same week that 'Dry Your Eyes ...' did.

An almost unbelievable double triumph.

As a sure sign that Mike's music was now part of the oxygen that the British public breathed, more cynical media observers suggested – wrongly and unfairly – that 'Dry Your Eyes' had deliberately been held back from release in anticipation of the by-now almost inevitable failure of the 'we're going to win this time' England football team at the Euro 2004 Championships. Beckham's XI, when not distracted by the alleged extra-curricular activities of their captain, manager, and numerous other key personnel, did fail. Skinner's single did sum up the nation's mood, not quite as did his namesake Frank Skinner's 'Three Lions', but sufficiently enough to provide a welcome extra fillip to sales. Intentional? No. Helpful? Yes. Were England ever going to win? No.

The year 2004 also saw its fair share of 'reply' records, a weird phenomenon whereby a hit record is followed by another song which claims to be in answer to the original. Pushing the boundaries of linguistic evolution to the limit, Eamon's delightfully titled 'Fuck You' enjoyed Number 1 status for weeks partly because of, rather than despite, the fact it contained the 'sounds-like-muck' four-letter friend being used almost forty times. Cue the spurned woman's retort, the equally splendid 'F.U.R.B.' by FURB. They even purported to be genuine former lovers.

So, it was perhaps not surprising when a song filtered through on to various radio stations – not least Radio 1's Scott Mills Show – touted as a riposte to Mr.Skinner. Everyone loved Mike's song, no one loved the 'reply'. It sank pretty much without trace. Supposedly, Mills was inundated with complaints about the record, but maybe people should just lighten up.

Another unforeseen aside from the success of 'Dry Your Eyes' was a claim made by a man named Michael Gagliano in *The Sun* that the single was very similar to

> *"Observers fuelled rumours that he was putting out tracks under pseudonyms, perhaps serving his penchant for anonymity well."*

his own song, 'Yesterday And Today Pt1', released under the name Epic in 2003. Gagliano is better known for playing George Harrison in The Counterfeit Beatles, one of the world's biggest Beatles tribute bands, as well as having a publishing deal with American label Rainbow. He said he was listening to the radio one day when he was startled to hear a song which he felt was very similar to his own. *The Sun* quoted him as saying, '(I) will be looking into the question of getting royalties from The Streets. To be honest, the money isn't an issue for me, I got into this game for the women. I would be happy if The Streets would give me the acknowledgment I deserve and credit me on the sleevenotes for the record.' Skinner's spokesperson later refuted the claim, saying to the press that Mike had 'never heard the other song' and that 'the strings in The Streets' single were taken from a sample CD which provides royalty free samples for artists. This is standard practice nowadays ... Obviously, Mike has never heard the other song in question. Apparently it was released towards the end of 2003, and 'Dry Your Eyes' was recorded as early as March 2003 and CDs of the track have been kicking around the label and people involved ever since. We have no idea how the other artist thinks Mike heard his music before recording it and find it all a bit strange.'

It wasn't just a case of answering claims about his material. Other media observers fuelled rumours that he was putting out tracks under pseudonyms, perhaps serving his penchant for anonymity well. For example, in June 2003, the music papers reported that The Streets was suspected of actually being behind a song called 'What Is The Problem?', supposedly by a previously unknown act called Grafiti. The story was that the 'big-time Italian producer' was actually Mike Skinner. The evidence was the obvious influence of The Streets and the under-rated Audio Bullys. What's more, they said, Skinner's music publisher was the very same as Grafiti's, they were both on the same label, and according to *NME*, 'to the astute ear, Skinner can be clearly heard singing backing vocals on the track.' Although the parent company, WEA, also issued a denial, the gossip was furthered by *NME* countering with two unnamed sources 'close to the record label [who] have confirmed that Mike Skinner is Grafiti, though they wish to remain anonymous.' Skinner's spokesman also denied it flatly, but it is a sure sign of an artist's popularity that instead of struggling to get his material heard at all, he is forced to deny ownership of numerous songs which possibly have nothing whatsoever to do with him.

In a move which once again paralleled Essex tribe The Prodigy, The Streets' next single 'Blinded By The Lights' came with a video that was banned from most TV stations because of its explicit content. The promo for the album's third single chronicled Skinner's night out at a wedding reception and contained scenes of drink and drug-induced violence, mobile-phone-filmed

> *"The video was banned and chastised by various bodies, with Ofcom saying it was not suitable for most mainstream pre-watershed channels."*

oral sex and general excess, climaxing with Skinner himself being beaten and left in a pool of blood.

The video was banned and chastised by various bodies, with Ofcom saying it was not suitable for most mainstream pre-watershed channels. The footage was directed by Adam Smith, who told NME.COM: 'It was hard work. Mike said he really didn't want to set it in a club, as he felt it had all been done. He wanted to do this whole suspense thing as well so I decided on a wedding. I tried to interweave the film with the narrative so it still made sense with the story of the album as well.'

Similarly, The Prodigy followed ultra-commercial smashes like 'Firestarter' and 'Breathe' with the highly controversial 'Smack My Bitch Up' single, whose video contained scenes of drugging, strippers, explicit sex scenes and fighting (all by a girl), and was likewise banned by virtually every TV station worth its moral high ground.

Both acts, at the same time, successfully redrew the lines surrounding their image and public perception using just such brutal visual tools.

CHAPTER 10:
THE STREETS ARE ALIVE WITH THE SOUND OF MUSIC

'Maybe my audiences can enjoy my music more if they think I am destroying myself.'

Not Mike Skinner. Janis Joplin.

'Generally, the best bet [at a Streets gig] is booze. Lots of it. If you bring the beer, we'll bring the party. In America, we're like the pissed blokes paraded in front. But in England, we're not as pissed as the people in the audience. I throw cans into the audience when I'm drunk, which is good – give some beer love – but every now and then someone gets twazipped on the head. Likewise, I've been smacked in the head by full cans, so I've paid my dues.'

117

Mike Skinner trying to sell The Streets live experience to Middle America, speaking to *Rolling Stone* in 2003.

Welchy is a plasterer. When he's finished, it's like a sheet of glass. So he says.

'Fuck me, Jimmy, I went to see The Streets last week. Scared shitless I was.'

'Why?'

'Well, there were loads of pissed up blokes getting lairy ... I spent most of the night looking at the floor ...'

Notably, some people suggested Mike was initially reluctant to tour The Streets as a live band at all, and was instead quite happy to just write music for release. In the light of his success with both albums, the commercial pressure to tour would have simply been too great, but it might be a sign of things to come should Skinner ever tire of life on the road.

But he did take to the road, albeit with at times mixed results ... for now.

If this book was to suggest that seeing The Streets live was not quite as mind-blowing as listening to any of his records, it would not be the first time this chink in the armour had been highlighted. The media are always looking for evidence of the Emperor's new clothes, and some feel that in Mike's live show they have their angle. The ever-objective and knowledgeable Krissi Murrison of *NME* refused to be swayed by the fawning media coverage of Mike and had this to say about his Carling Weekend performance: 'The Streets have new material up their sleeves. Unfortunately, unlike The Strokes, Mike Skinner's is pretty lacklustre. Where his wide-boy charisma was once a welcome relief from faux-ghetto bluster and art-school drop-out mumblings, a year and a half down the line he may have new songs but he's still without any new gags.' When you are performing on stage with Blur, The Strokes, Beck and Doves, there is not much room for error. In such circumstances, the unforgiving torch of comparison is glaringly bright.

"I think I'm quite a funny bloke, but I'm no Frank Sinatra. Onstage we try and respect the fact that I'm not a great performer by getting really drunk and having a really good party."

Of course, Skinner also airs his own reservations. 'I don't really pay much attention to the live stuff. It's a skill to sing, really. I think I'm quite a funny bloke, but I'm no Frank Sinatra. Onstage we try and respect the fact that I'm not a great performer by getting really drunk and having a really good party. And … I don't practice.' He is too busy writing and recording music. Which is fair enough. People do sometimes have the annoying habit of saying things behind your back that are absolutely true.

But in a way, what did you expect? This is a man whose average song has more words than most albums. He is a one-man tour de force, albeit with numerous partners in crime, but this is not Wu Tang or So Solid. Relying so heavily on street wit and rapier sharp observations is always going to get diluted in front of four, ten or fifty thousand lager-swilling gig-goers.

Although hip-hop is Skinner's raison d'etre, it is punk that stabs you in the ears when you see him live. Despite this anarchic heritage, there are signs that Skinner is starting to want to improve matters out on the road. Speaking in *The Sun* in March 2005, he revealed that having played his first ever gig totally sober, he was delighted with the results. 'I got to the point where it was getting absolutely ridiculous ... when you start insulting the audience like I was doing, it doesn't go down too well.'

"Skinner does still have a certain verve on stage, however."

His live band have had their fair share of weird experiences too. At the 2004 V Festival, rock-gods Muse found themselves a duo, not trio, when bassist Chris Wolstenholme was injured and unable to play. Cue a most bizarre marriage as The Streets' live bassist Morgan Nicholls learnt Matt Bellamy & Co.'s entire set in four days to save their pomp rock blushes.

Only a few days later at Reading, Nicholls was himself in a pickle when his own bass was mistakenly left behind in Leeds from the previous night's show! Fortunately, Neil Mahoney from Amplifier lent Nicholls his own four-string for The Streets' important main stage performance.

Skinner does still have a certain verve on stage, however. For one tour, he asked fans to email him their best/worst drunken videos, which he wanted to use as a giant visual backdrop to his live show. The email given was: imneverdrinkingagain@thestreets.co.uk. He also offered a free Streets cigarette lighter to fans who got three or more friends to download The Streets' logo for their mobiles; better still, he put some hilarious footage on the internet of himself trying vainly and comically to set up 'the very first Streets' drum kit', filmed by his very own DV hand-held camera.

And how does he choose some of these dates and venues? Well, in the spring of 2005 he made no secret of wanting to play in Ibiza, nothing massive, just a show to get himself and his band a free holiday. Priceless.

> ## *"The origins of the word 'chav' are disputed but the most likely answer is some derivation of a gypsy word for children, 'chavvy'."*

2004 was the Year of the Chav. It must have been, because Chav-bible *The Sun* said so. What's in a name? Chav ... More easily defined by its star followers than its socio-economic demograph (although some twats have tried to do this, more of which later), the religion of the chav probably has substantially more followers than the Church of England.

The origins of the word 'chav' are disputed but the most likely answer is some derivation of a gypsy word for children, 'chavvy'. This word also dripped into south London vernacular, again to be used for children, although it can also be used as a term of derision, when an adult is a chav, namely a kid and therefore not worthy.

Some people believe the term evolved around Chatham in Kent, with locals calling certain types chavs because of the way they dressed.

Who knows when the first chavs existed. In a Sky One documentary, Julie Burchill traced the social roots of the phenomenon back as far as the 1940s and earlier, whining on about the manufacturing economy and 'headlines of hate'. She placed the chav as a creature wholly wrapped up in a class confrontation against what she called 'the bland' middle-classes.

One of the few interesting aspects of the programme was the suggestion that the very first chav was Sir Jimmy Saville. He was wearing gold lame tracksuits over forty years before the new Millennial chav made them popular again, his bling-rating is up there with 50 Cent, albeit gold and, in his words, 'fake', and his general love of all things garish would certainly earmark him as the great-grandfather of the chav. Notably, he wore the trackies not to make some banal and out-dated class statement, but because it was 'convenient'.

The list of other famous chavs is endless: Britney Spears is right up there, with her 'Pimps' wedding outfits, her shambolically-dressed groom, her Louis Vitton upholstered Hummer army utility vehicle (beautifully and tactfully used in her 'Do Somethin' video while American troops were still being killed daily driving them in Iraq), her designer clothing for her pooch and the hair extensions straight out of Claire's Accessories (well, alright, probably not, but you know what I mean). David Beckham, Kate Moss (who models for chav Uber-label Burberry) and Jordan are all considered by many to be fine examples of the celeb chav. Prince Harry is definitely a chav, no question. So is the magnificent Vicky Pollard, hyper-fast-talking star of *Little Britain* − a character actually based on a young teenage boy that David Walliams once met. Her sovereign rings, 'half pineapple' hair and pink tracksuits perfectly captured the look for thousands of females. Even the Blairs have been spotted showing flashes of Burberry. The brilliantly gifted Wayne Rooney, football prodigy and Shrek-lookalike took the pressure off being perceived as the man to win England the World Cup/ Euro Championships/anything-we-would-otherwise-

"Burberry was the label of choice. Some pubs actually started to refuse to serve anyone wearing the famous checkered patterns."

get-knocked-out-of, by holidaying in Paris, photographed on a bus stop bench in a woolly hat, donkey jacket and jeans. The media frequently cited Lotto winner Michael Carroll as an example of 'when chavs go wrong'. Despite winning £9.7 million, Carroll spent his £10,000 a week in interest with a stock-car track in his garden and paying to get to numerous court appearances.

Burberry was the label of choice. Some pubs actually started to refuse to serve anyone wearing the famous checkered patterns. The countless dictionaries on book shop shelves all acknowledged the word 'chav' as a new buzzword for 2004. Chunky jewellery, bracelets, baseball caps, tracksuits, and 'wacky' mobile phone covers were also chav-prerequisites. Ferocious dogs suddenly became very popular, especially American pit bull terriers. There was even a spoof version of the world's most famous board-game, named Chavopoloy, complete with squares for White Lightning booze, Kwik Save or Aldi's and the bonus square, 'Collect Your Giro as you Pass Go!'

Then of course there was the 'bangin' 'oliday'. Ibiza, Falaraki, any island where your parents can't be contacted and booze is cheap. English breakfasts, football shirts, preferably a Sky One 'reality' show film crew and suitcases full of condoms (or not). So, chavs marched triumphantly around the globe, well, at least much of Europe, spreading the gospel like a marauding missionary (position).

> *"Any self-respecting chav is too busy being ... a chav, to make a documentary about it. It's a way of life, not a social thesis."*

No self-respecting social phenomenon worth its salt (and vinegar) fails to infect the music world. Chav did so with a vengeance. The most obvious example was oddball Welsh rap act, Goldie Lookin' Chain. Their hilarious songs, comic videos and classic chav dress-sense made them obvious candidates but it was their Burberry-painted 'Chavalier' that took the crown. The humourous website chavscum.co.uk (chavspotting.com is another similar site) stated that chavs only listened to three genres, rap, R&B and dance, preferably only from the Top 40. Then, according to those that 'know', there was Mike Skinner ...

The tie-ins were easy. The barbed wire bracelet – a little unfair, as this unique piece of jewellery was hand-made for him by his sister (Skinner repeatedly had to deny its design was all about 'self-hate', explaining that it was just a cool design); the clothes, Ellesse, Nike, Adidas trackies, Fred Perry's etc; the songs' subject matter – you know which bits; his dog; even his own album artwork seemed to fit the bill.

But let's face it, it's not the nicest thing to say about someone, calling them a chav. Journalist Julie Burchill actually went on for an hour in her documentary saying she was proud to be a chav – including the nauseating closing line, 'don't hate us because we are beautiful', but really, come on, any self-respecting chav is too busy being … a chav, to make a documentary about it. It's a way of life, not a social thesis. Besides, many people don't take too well being called a chav, whereas others seem to boast about it.

Besides, chavs had been around for decades, just in different guises. Blur had a phase when they would have perfectly fitted the bill. Harry Enfield's 'Loadsamoney' character had certain aspects even back in the 80s. Track-suited clans have roamed the streets for years and years, ever since the 'casuals' of the late Seventies/early Eighties made unaffordable designer labels the ultimate must-have item, even for school kids. Saying gold sovereign jewellery is a new fashion is tantamount to sacrilege in certain parts of the East End. It's all been around before, just not under the 'chav' banner.

So, for Mike Skinner to be called a chav, or at least a chav's choice of musician, is perhaps unfortunate. Having said that, there were so many other comparisons being made – Chekhov, Shakespeare, etc – I am sure he could live with a few rather more salubrious ones.

What Skinner's 'chav' tag did show (whether deservedly awarded or not), however, is the massive extent to which The Streets had connected with the great British public. *The Sun* talked about Skinner without explaining or introducing him, a sure sign that at least its own loyal four million-plus daily readers knew exactly who he was. For such a huge subculture –

"Maybe he was shrinking back into the dimly lit railway arches and dank side streets from whence he had emerged."

whether you agree with its simplistic summary above or not – to identify with Skinner, and to buy his records in such enormous volume was a final confirmation that by 2005, he was indeed a 'household name'.

In the light of such a public profile, Skinner grew visibly more uncomfortable. He seemed to start to do less interviews, be seen at less and less music parties/ ceremonies, noticeably shirk the limelight. Skinner is renowned for rejecting publicity, shunning awards ceremonies such as The Brits and the Ivor Novello Awards, where he won Best Contemporary Song for 'Weak Become Heroes'. Although his website continued to be one of the most innovative and interesting music sites on the net, this medium is always going to be a technological veil or screen protecting him from too much first-hand contact. Maybe he was shrinking back into the dimly lit railway arches and dank side streets from whence he had emerged.

CHAPTER 11:
DON'T BLAME IT ON THE SUNSHINE, BLAME IT ON THE GERI

'You still see him on the tube picking his nose. He's not one of those limousine guys.'
Teddy Hanson of The Mitchell Brothers.

Mike Skinner admitted that after *Original Pirate Material*, he went a bit 'George Best', and similarly, after the even more substantial success of *A Grand* ... he explained, with alarming honesty, how he had become heavily interested in gambling. Speaking to the media, he said he had spent tens of thousands of pounds on betting sessions. He has since categorically denied that he has a gambling problem, but it is easy to see why the newspapers would find this angle intriguing. Bizarrely, he even took his penchant abroad with near disastrous consequences: 'Basically, I was getting too drunk and betting lots of money. The US tour was nearly pulled halfway through because I lost the tour cash float in the casino. I was even getting in to spread betting. It's scary. I've lost a lot.' He was apparently at his lowest ebb around July 2004 – ironically the same month that both his second album and 'Dry Your Eyes ...' single were topping the charts, namely when his life was about to get even more hectic. Fortunately, he was able to realise the dangers of excessive gambling and has put a stop to it: 'I haven't touched anything since ...' You can almost picture his cheeky grin when he also said, 'But hey, I'm a reasonably successful musician. I was bound to go through that at some stage.'

With heavenly timing, his second album was selling by the truckload. Eventually, sales by the end of 2004 would surpass one million also, with no sign of letting up Skinner had entered that supergroup of British artists who can sell albums in the home territory in the seven figures. Nothing would ever be the same for him again – as for gambling, he would have to spend a lot of time with a stubby pencil and a betting slip thrown into the bin to burn a hole in the fortune which he is now poised to accumulate.

It will be interesting to see – particularly in light of the multi-million pound film deals he is said to have been offered – how Mike will react to this new-found super-wealth. What is perhaps so refreshing is that after a massively successful debut album, many sophomore records merely document how isolated and 'weird' the writer's life has become as a result of that success. *A Grand ...* did nothing of the sort, it was just Mikey out on the town again, absolutely nothing seemed to have changed. For Skinner, this was perfectly natural. After the success of his debut, he explained, he had an awful lot of nights out. The follow-up album took two years to make and that equated to a lot of nights on the tiles.

He seems determined not to fall into this trap in future either. He has no aspirations to suddenly start populating the VIP rooms of superclubs and only sipping Kristal. 'I don't know much about the celebrity lifestyle, coz I haven't really done it. Now and then, sumfink

> *"I lost the tour cash float in the casino.*
> *I was even getting in to spread betting.*
> *It's scary. I've lost a lot."*

comes up that you think will be a good laugh, but it's never as good as you expect. I've got a really big family, so I just go and relax with them and go out with my mates.'

Yet, his observations mentioned earlier in this book about hip-hop superstars becoming distanced from their environmental and social roots is entirely valid; however, he is now on the verge of that same paradox. Being devoid of the very lifestyle that made him famous. It is unlikely that he will continue to be able to go to his local pub for a quiet drink (or a loud one) for much longer. He will not 'holiday with me mates' anywhere near a public resort. He won't be able to. Like it or not, Mike Skinner is now a bona fide superstar. How that affects his muse and his incredibly gifted writing ability will be a fascinating development to watch.

Geri Spice is to blame. She came on stage out of a sixty foot pair of women's legs, 'birthed' if you will, like some pop bastard. Before that we had to endure the awful spectacle of Michael Jackson's 'crucifix-like' pose while singing 'Earth Song', an aural and visual torture that was only ended when Jarvis Cocker saved the nation with his bum-wiggling antics (he still hasn't got an MBE for that … must be red tape). Countless dull 'megastars' have bestowed the Brits with performances that seek to spend more budget than a small African nation's GDP, but few

> *"Skinner stood almost on the cameraman's lens, alongside Calvin, brilliantly playing to a far bigger and more important crowd… the television viewers."*

have actually given us anything worth watching. There was The Darkness in 2004 of course, on a rising column as phallic as the Empire State on Viagra, but hey, it's The Darkness, what do you expect? Of course they overdid it, that's the whole point with that band. Thankfully. But they are the exception to the rule. Generally, the Brits performances are a shallow, self-indulgent celebrity wank-fest. Robbie Williams anyone?

Enter The Streets.

Despite his prediction that The Streets would always be a 'cult classic', the music industry held a very different opinion. When the nominations for the prestigious Brit Awards were announced, Mike Skinner and his cohorts were nominated for four gongs, among them 'Best British Male', 'Best British Album' and 'Best British Single' (for 'Dry Your Eyes').

At the 2005 Brit Awards, his performance was a masterpiece. As mentioned, by his own admission, he was not going to win 'Best Live Act', but his strategy was, at the risk of losing myself up his arse, genius. Instead of playing to the massed ranks of the back-slapping, champagne-swilling executives of the British record industry – numbering approximately 3000 if you include the 'lucky' few punters – Skinner stood almost on the cameraman's lens, alongside Calvin, brilliantly playing to a far bigger and more important crowd... the television viewers, numbering approximately *eight million*.

At first his rendition of 'Dry Your Eyes' sounded harsh, odd, 'not like the single'. But then it grew on you ... fast. You realised what he was doing. For those few minutes, your Chav-must-have plasma screen was filled with his face, larger-than-life, in your lounge, in your face. He looked genuinely troubled by the words spilling out of his mouth. You had forgotten the Brit Awards and were listening to his sorry tale. He had grown his hair since the last time we'd seen him on telly, almost like he'd stopped bothering to shave. His eyes fixed, staring, his gait was slightly nervous but endearing. He looked fantastic. There was no bling, there was no 'hydraulically-ground-breaking' platform, 60-piece ensemble, semi-naked dancers or world-first pyrotechnics. Just him, Calvin and a tale of a girl he had lost. Coming on the same show as Robbie Williams and Joss Stone ('Best Urban', naturally, coming from Devon and recording in the USA) it seemed like he'd reclaimed British music from the realms of pitiful self-indulgence.

The Brit Awards are an essential part of the British music calendar, for all their faults, and winning one will undoubtedly change an artist's career. Mike didn't collect his award for 'Best British Male'. His mate did. By now, it was no surprise.

His mate said, 'the last I saw of him he was heading to the toilet ...'

... And out on tour. Throughout January and February of 2005, The Streets hit the road for a series of highly anticipated live shows. The Brit Award win slap bang in

"The last I saw of him he was heading to the toilet ..."

the middle of these shows only heightened the frenzy around the gigs which were, needless to say, a total sell-out. Supporting the main act was The Mitchell Brothers – no, not 'Graaant,' or Phil from *Eastenders* (although both were on sabbaticals from the soap so who knows?), but the first signing to Mike Skinner's very own record label known as The Beats. Working with them in early 2005, Skinner hinted that the fruits of their labours sounded like a hybrid of Outkast and 'Don't Mug Yourself'! The then-underground star (shortly to enter the charts in March 2005) Kano also worked with the duo.

Set up to introduce artists whom Skinner thought should be heard, this so-called 'boutique' label was not a new idea – Limp Bizkit's Fred Durst has done it, Puff Daddy has done it, Madonna did it with Maverick, signing The Prodigy in the US and Alanis Morrisette – who you may have not heard of but she released the biggest selling debut album by a female ever, the 35-million-selling *Jagged Little Pill*. Oh, and that beat combo from Liverpool did it and named the label after a fruit. So, let's face it, it works.

The signing of its first act was not without its hitches, however. The story goes that when Skinner met up with the Mitchell Brothers to put their signatures on the contract from his new record label, they started to share a few beers – when a lawyer later phoned to ask after the signed paperwork, Mike allegedly didn't know where it was! New contracts had to be drawn up and re-signed.

CHAPTER 12:
THE TOADFISH
AND THE FUTURE

'When you start off, you sound like shit. Then you get better. And when you get better, people start showing interest in your older work. There's no lost genius really. You'd just find music that's not as good as the music that I'm making now.'

Mike Skinner.

Eminem in a film? It would never work. Following in a magic/tragic line of pop stars-turned-actors/actresses, numerous rumours have Mike Skinner being offered multi-million pound film deals. Some say they are for *8 Mile*-style fictionalisations of his life, others pure fiction. As far back as the summer of 2003, Mike was teasing the music press by saying that there wouldn't even be a second album, 'It's all over, finished. I'm making a film!' He was only ribbing of course. Despite a swathe of offers which, according to Mike, 'all want to put me in a modern day *Quadrophenia* or something,' he was not tempted. Besides, he added, he can't act …

… Unlike Toadfish from *Neighbours*, one of Skinner's heroes. When Mike toured Down Under for the 2005 Big Day Out, his most treasured memory was going on

"I was quite embarrassed when I met Toadfish."

to the long-running soap's set at the Melbourne studios and meeting Ryan Maloney who plays the part of 'the Toad', aka Jarrod Rebecchi. 'That was quite strange" he told *Undercover News*. "I couldn't stop laughing because I was actually quite star struck. I've met a lot of famous people, but I was quite embarrassed when I met Toadfish.'

With the multi-million record sales, countless awards and endless accolades, no doubt Mike Skinner will abandon his roots and be found taking nine years to record another album, this time in a 'residential' studio somewhere in Wales with a bottle of Kristal and a duck-feather pillow for comfort. Not.

Speaking in 2005, it was clear where his priorities still lay. Music. 'I still do it in my bedroom! I've got a lot of other rooms now, but I still do it in the bedroom. Being close to bed means you can get up in the middle of the night and get on with stuff.'

He still texts himself lyrics and ideas. He still writes at home mostly. He admits much of *A Grand* ... was written after beery nights out ("Don't Mug Yourself ... hammered when we did that and I think it's better for it!'). He shuns writing while stoned, saying it blunts your creativity and although the material may sound good at the time, in the cold light of the next morning it is worthless. His typical day is spent 'waking up without an

"The first three hours of the day my brain is on fire!"

alarm, writing 'til I feel sleepy,' he told *Notion* magazine. 'Then I probably go to bed for an hour ... it sounds lazy but I get a lot more done that way. The first three hours of the day my brain is on fire!'

He seems to have changed little.

But things around him have changed ... a lot. Whereas after his first album he was spotted in the street (no pun intended) quite a lot, generally with some supportive comment from a music fan, after the huge success of his second album, he acknowledges that the level of fame he now resides in has increased exponentially. 'You get used to people walking past and doing a double take,' he continued, 'but this is more. Sometimes it gets to the point where it's scary, very scary.'

Talking to *NME*, he said with admirable frankness,

'I live in Stockwell and walking to the tube is still exactly the same as walking to the tube ever was and going to the shop at midnight to get fags is no different, nothing is different. I'm as street as I've ever been because I still live in the same city and I still do the same things. I've just got a nicer floor and nicer wallpaper and I've got a telly in my kitchen now.'

For now, this is the world which he inhabits.

"However, reluctantly or not, bodyguards, schedules, magazine front covers, the spectre of internet leaks of new material, press intrusion, this is also part of his world now."

However, reluctantly or not, bodyguards, schedules, magazine front covers, the spectre of internet leaks of new material, press intrusion, this is also part of his world now. The harsh reality is that Skinner will not be able to walk 'the streets' at will for ever. Fact.

Mind you, there are perks. 'It's getting to the stage where things are a bit more like that rock and roll dream. The money gets better, my attractiveness to the opposite sex is getting better ... after a couple of Top Ten hits, suddenly I'm very attractive!'

He says he is 'not going to base my whole career on audio books ...' suggesting a definite move away from the material on his first two albums perhaps, but as ever, who knows what his next move might be.

While I was writing this book, I got a letter from the Credit Controller of a very large mail order stationery company. It said I had an invoice that was overdue. It was a very nice letter, well-written and polite. It was from a man called Mike Skinner.

Is there no end to this man's talents?

EPILOGUE

'Hello, is that Record Finders? Yes, I wonder if ... yes, I'll hold ... ('Smoke On The Water' plays on the crackly line) Hello? Yes, I wondered if you can track down a copy of Cliff Richard's 'Devil Woman'... er, no, it's not for me, it's for my mom ... honest.'

SOURCE
ACKNOWLEDGEMENTS

The following magazines and websites were invaluable in compiling this work:

There are thousands of articles on Mike Skinner and The Streets, but a few are worthy of special mention: Ben Thompson's piece in *The Observer* on Sunday April 25, 2004 is a definitive inside look at the man; likewise, Richard Jinman's excellent piece in *The Guardian* on Friday February 4, 2005; Ray Rogers' on-line article for Brant Publications Inc. is superb; Simon Reynold's *Energy Flash* was also an excellent reference for garage history as was the website ukflex.com and their MC Pages, plus James Huggett's work in *The Village Voice*. And finally, anything by Krissi Murrison.

Xfm, NME.com, Gil Kaufman and MTV, MTV.com, Corey Moss, *The Guardian,* Alex Petridis, *The Observer*, Q magazine, *Rolling Stone,* Austin Scaggs, David Merryweather, *Drowned in Sound,* Amazon.co.uk, *CDNow,* *CMJ* magazine and website, Brad Maybe, Gigwise.com website, Ted Kessler and Dan Martin.

Although this is not an official nor authorised history of The Streets and Mike Skinner, I must thoroughly recommend that anyone interested in the band should visit the official website: www.the-streets.co.uk which is innovative, entertaining and informative.

ALSO AVAILABLE FROM INDEPENDENT MUSIC PRESS...

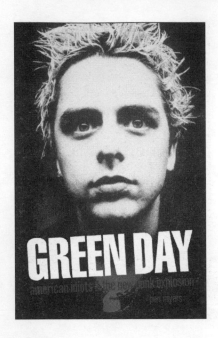

GREEN DAY: AMERICAN IDIOTS AND THE NEW PUNK EXPLOSION
by Ben Myers

The world's first and only full biography of Green Day. Self-confessed latch-key kids from small blue-collar Californian towns, Green Day have gone on to sell 50 million albums and single-handedly redefine the punk and rock genre for an entire generation. Inspired by both the energy of British punk bands as well as cult American groups, Green Day gigged relentlessly across the US underground before eventually signing to Warners and releasing their 1994 major label debut *Dookie*, which was a 10-million-selling worldwide hit album. With the arrival of Green Day, suddenly music was dumb, fun, upbeat and colourful again. Many now credit the band with saving rock from the hands of a hundred grunge-lite acts. In 2004 Green Day reached a career pinnacle with the concept album *American Idiot*, a sophisticated commentary on modern life - not least their dissatisfaction with their president. Myers is an authority on punk and hardcore and in this unauthorised book charts the band members' difficult childhoods and their rise to success, speaking to key members of the punk underground and music industry figures along the way.

ISBN 0 9539942 9 5 208 Pages Paperback, 8pp b/w pics £12.99 World Rights

For more information please visit www.impbooks.com

THE EIGHT LEGGED ATOMIC DUSTBIN
WILL EAT ITSELF
by Martin Roach

A fully updated, revised and expanded edition of the book that *Vox* magazine called 'a phenomenon' on its publication in 1992. With all three of the Stourbridge bands – The Wonder Stuff, Pop Will Eat Itself and Ned's Atomic Dustbin – having reformed in 2004, largely due to public demand, this book brings the history of this unique music scene up to date. Extensive interviews with band members reveal what they have been up to throughout the thirteen years since this book's first publication, including writing Hollywood soundtracks and running record companies. A comprehensive chronicle of all their record releases to date and massive histories of each band complete the third edition of this publishing classic. Originally printed in 1992 as I.M.P.'s first ever title, the original 'blue' edition sold over 5,000 copies - predominantly out of carrier bags outside gigs and at festivals! The second 'red' edition was released to the book trade and sold a further 3,000 copies and both are now collectors' items among the fanbase.

ISBN 0 9549704 0 3 176 Pages Paperback, 45pp b/w pics £8.99 World Rights

For more information please visit www.impbooks.com

MUSE: INSIDE THE MUSCLE MUSEUM
by Ben Myers

The first and only biography of one of the most innovative and successful rock bands of recent years. Formed in the mid-1990s in a sleepy sea-side Devonshire town, Muse comprises teenage friends Matt Bellamy, Chris Wolstenholme and Dominic Howard. 2001's *Origin Of Symmetry* album spawned Top 10 hits such as 'Plug-In Baby' and a unique version of Nina Simone's classic, 'Feeling Good'. Their third album, *Absolution*, entered the UK charts at Number 1 in October 2003 – by then, all the signs were there that Muse were on the verge of becoming one of the biggest bands of the new century. Throughout 2004, they won over countless new fans at festivals, including a now-famous headline slot at Glastonbury, which preceded a two-night sell-out of the cavernous Earl's Court and a Brit Award for 'Best Live Act' in early 2005. This book tells that full story right from their inception and includes interviews conducted both with the band and those who have witnessed their climb to the top - a position they show no sign of relinquishing any time soon.

ISBN 0 9539942 6 0   208 Pages   Paperback, 8pp b/w pics   £12.99   World Rights

For more information please visit www.impbooks.com

SENT FROM COVENTRY
TWO TONE'S CHEQUERED PAST
by Richard Eddington

The first detailed analysis and history of the music phenomenon called Two Tone, a movement led by bands such as The Specials, The Selecter, Bad Manners, Madness and The Beat. *Sent From Coventry* examines the early years of the characters central to the embryonic Two Tone scene set in a grainy, monochrome world of pre-Thatcherite Britain. The author was at the heart of the scene and regularly found himself in the company of key individuals, and is therefore perfectly placed to chronicle this most fascinating of movements. Includes previously unseen photographs from the private collections of band members.

ISBN 0 9539942 5 2   256 Pages   Paperback, b/w pics   £12.99   World Rights

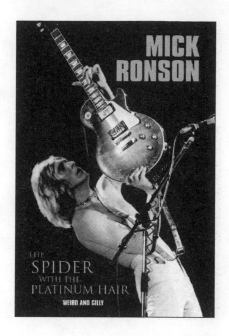
For more information please visit www.impbooks.com

BIKERS: LEGEND, LEGACY AND LIFE
By Gary Charles

A painstakingly detailed chronicle of a unique band of nomadic desperado, a full circuit tour of the domain of the life-style Biker. Trawling deep into history to detail the early town-sieges of America's mid-West in the '40s, through to the British Mod and Rocker coastal clashes of the '60s, the Easy Riders of the '70s to the Street Fighters of the 21st Century, this book offers the definitive insight into Biker culture.

Gary Charles is a global expert in his field and has unparalleled knowledge of the history and intricacies of the biker universe, plus access to an astounding archive of photographs spanning decades of lifestyle biker events.

ISBN: 0 9539942 2 8 128 Pages Paperback, b/w pics £9.99 World Rights

For more information please visit www.impbooks.com

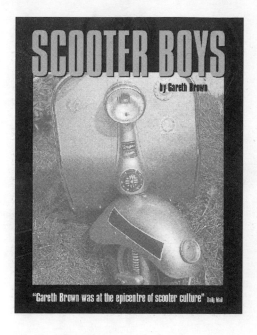

SKINS By Gavin Watson

Perhaps one of the most reviled yet misunderstood of all the youth subcultures, the skinhead look originated back in the 60s as a simple fashion statement. Sartorially proud of their working class roots, the original skinhead was a multi-cultural, politically broad-minded individual. The 70s saw the look adopted by the legions of right-wing extremists and for many years was a fashion pariah. Towards the end of the 90s, the closely cropped look has been championed by a new generation of celebrities, bringing skinhead style back into the mainstream once again.

Gavin Watson's critically acclaimed work is widely acknowledged as a classic photograph archive of historical value.

"A modern classic." **The Times**

ISBN 0 9539942 1 X 128 Pages Paperback, b/w pics £9.99 World Rights

For more information please visit www.impbooks.com